Attack of the Killer Banana

How I handled my extremely fussy eater

Shannon Thiry

Published by Shannon Thiry
www.shannonthiry.com

Book Layout © 2017 BookDesignTemplates.com

Attack of the Killer Banana / Shannon Thiry. -- 1st ed.
ISBN 978-0-9944975-5-0

For my mum, thanks for infecting me with your love of learning. And for William and Rachael, the best kids a mum could hope for.

If there is a book you want to read,
But it hasn't been written yet,
Then you must write it.

—TONI MORRISON

CONTENTS

Introduction

From the time that I learned to read, books have been my 'go to' place. Whether it's to learn something new or just to get lost in someone else's imagination, I love that feeling of connection that books bring. I felt quite secure in the world knowing that if I had a problem, however big or small, there would be a book out there, somewhere, just waiting to give me an answer.

When I first started to realise that my son's fussy eating was more intense than most children's, of course I searched the internet and the library catalogues for a book that would connect me to what I was experiencing. I looked for 'the' book that was going to make all my confusion vanish under the bright glow of enlightenment. When I couldn't find that book I looked for any information that would tell me what I could do to fix his fussy eating.

The truth is that I did find plenty of information on feeding fussy children but the more I read the worse I felt. You see, the problem wasn't, as I had thought, that

William was fussy. Oh, no. Clearly the problem was that I was an idiot: a useless mother incapable of setting boundaries and keeping routines. I know that's not what the parenting books and child health websites actually say, but, oh my goodness, do they imply it!

So pervasive is this belief that parents have the ability to cause and also fix their children's fussy eating, that it is very difficult to find a book, or a website, or even a pamphlet that suggests anything else. I wanted empathy and reassurance but all I could find was a list of things I was doing wrong.

After many failed attempts to find the book I was searching for I finally realised that the book that I really needed didn't exist. I did eventually find the help that I needed. I did get answers. I also realised that there were a lot of other parents out there really struggling to get their kids to eat. But still there was no book. No delightful little compendium that you could throw in your handbag and read on the train or in-between loads of washing.

Finally, after much self-doubt and soul searching, I decided to write it myself. *Attack of the Killer Banana* is written for every mum or dad who has ever felt judged, condescended to, or just plain frustrated by their inability to get their child to eat.

My son William is a fussy eater. I have come across other terms for his condition, such as 'food neophobia' and 'picky eating'. But I will refer to this condition as fussy eating mainly because those were the words I would type into the internet search engine when I was trying to figure out what to do with this kid who refused to eat.

I understand that most children dabble with fussy eating and refusing to try new foods; I've been told that it's a normal aspect of child development. But William's fussiness was anything but normal. What started as him turning his head away and crying out in protest ended up with him running, screaming, from the room if you offered him the 'wrong' food, especially bananas.

William didn't always hate bananas. In fact, he liked them right up until an extreme weather event, Cyclone Larry, hit Far North Queensland in 2006 and interrupted banana supplies. The cyclone caused untold damage, destroying just about everything in its path, including about ninety per cent of Australia's banana crop. The price of bananas soared from around $3 per kilo to $14 per kilo in a matter of days.

We were mostly unaffected by the trauma facing our northern brothers and sisters. They had faced loss of life, loss of homes and loss of livelihoods. And I was put on banana rations. Actually, I just stopped buying them. By the time the prices had returned to normal, William had decided that he no longer liked them. I forgot to mention this fact to my sister when she babysat for us not long after that. Let's just say she was more than a bit taken aback when he started screaming hysterically at her after she innocently offered him a banana. It seemed that bananas had suddenly become his arch nemesis. Attack of the Killer Banana… *dun-dun-dun*!

It took me a long time to find books or information that held a message that wasn't just about blaming the parents for their children's fussy eating. I kept looking because, even though the doctors, nurses, parenting books, magazines and online articles were strongly implying that it was all my fault, I couldn't shake the feeling that it wasn't.

This feeling — that there was more to William's fussy eating — was reinforced when my daughter came along and confused things even more by being a good eater. I really didn't even have to try with her. You'd be forgiven for thinking this would make me feel better, but truly, I was just more confused. I had one child who ate well and another that screamed in terror at the suggestion of eating a banana, and all the literature and medical advice I could find at the time implied that it was my fault. But if it was *all* my fault then, logically, Rachael would be as bad at eating as William, wouldn't she? Only she wasn't; she really and truly wasn't. Where William would refuse pumpkin puree because of the tiniest, almost imperceptible fibres that most people wouldn't even notice, Rachael would demolish a whole bowl of pureed vegies *with* chicken *and* rice. Something beyond my understanding had to be going on here. I just had to keep looking.

It was exhausting and I was exhausted. I had all but given up on ever finding that crucial piece of the puzzle that would make it all make sense. And then one day I found it. Well, it was a hint really. A wisp of an idea that it might not be all my fault. It was the renewal I needed to not give up hope. Then the wisp turned into an actual solid idea and — oh my goodness — how good was it to feel that connection; to be heard and validated? I wasn't useless and William wasn't being a brat; he had a very real fear of food that would not be overcome by anger, bullying, punishment, coercion, bribery or any of the other standard strategies that I had been encouraged to use. There were issues at play in William's biology, and in my relationship with him, that needed a much deeper understanding of both the physical and psychological aspects of eating, child development and relationships.

We have been on quite a journey. We've been through a lot and learnt a lot and now we're ready to share it with the world, in this book.

For ages I wished that this could be a success story, a shining beacon held out to the lost and confused. I wished that, until I realised that success stories make me feel a little bit sick. It's not that I begrudge another person's success, because I don't. I'm really and truly happy for them. It's just that their success puts pressure on me to be successful too. Well-meaning people can hold up this 'proof of success' as evidence that if I were to just try a little harder, or persevere for a little bit longer, I, too, could experience success.

Those well-meaning people don't know what I know; they don't know that I don't have what it takes to change William and his phobia of food. They don't know how burnt out I am from failing all of the time. They don't know about my depression and anxiety, issues I am only just now beginning to get a handle on.

If you too have been walking this walk for a while, then rest assured, this is not a 'success' story, at least not in the conventional sense. I hope that you will find solidarity in these pages, a sense of not being alone. It's okay if you don't have what it takes, because neither do I.

Despite my own resignation, I am eternally optimistic on behalf of other parents whose children refuse to eat. I can't help but wonder if William's outcome might not have been different if I'd been able to read this book when we were starting our journey.

I fervently hope that this story might find you in the very early stages of your journey, where your hope has not been burnt out. I hope that you might not have journeyed very far into fussy eating, that you have not yet been broken by the constant rejection and too many failures, and that the things I have learnt might just be enough to help you out, or at least point you in the right direction.

If you're anything like me, it won't be enough to know why it's happening, or what to call it; you'll want to know how to fix it. Unfortunately this is a problem not easily solved, if it is, in fact, solvable. I have certainly not solved William's fussy eating, but I *am* on the way to understanding it. I haven't found a magic wand. I don't know all the answers. I like to think that what I have discovered, though, is an excellent place to start.

What Do you Mean, your Child Won't Eat?

You've heard that saying: 'you can lead a horse to water but you can't make him drink'? Well, I was leading a child to food and could not, for love or money, make him eat.

William's eating started out okay. His appetite was always small but by the time he was eight or nine months old he was eating vegetable purees, fruit purees, rice cereal and yogurt. By the time he was twelve months old he was also eating strawberries, blueberries and fresh snow peas from our garden. It was slow going but it wasn't anything to worry about.

It was when I started to increase the texture that things began to change. Slowly but surely he became pickier and pickier, refusing to eat more and more of the foods he had previously liked, and showing more and more resistance to trying new foods.

He had always taken a long time to feed even as an infant on breast or bottle, but my frustration increased as he moved from babyhood to toddlerhood and the foods I was presenting became more complex. He took forever to eat even the smallest of meals. Eons passed. Empires were built and destroyed in the time it took him to eat two bites of a fish finger, three peas and a kernel of corn. It became a struggle to find anything that he would eat — unless it was chocolate, chips, crackers or cake. But even these were often viewed with suspicion and could be dismissed on sight for no apparent reason.

When I say 'dismissed', let me be clear, there was no polite refusal, no, 'No thank you, mother', no, 'I'm not particularly fond of cake with coconut in it, but I'll try a chocolate chip biscuit'. There was screaming and crying, clamped lips and thrashing limbs. His reactions were totally out of proportion to the situation. It was almost as if he was afraid or terrified, but it didn't make any sense to me because people love to eat, right?

I wanted my child to eat well. I knew what the medical professionals and child health books said he 'should' be eating but I was at a complete and utter loss as to how I was going to get it in his mouth, let alone his tummy.

Maybe I should force him to eat? But how much force would it require? Short of sitting on him and forcing his jaws open and shoving the food in, I couldn't see how forcing him would work.

Maybe I should refuse to give him anything else to eat? Surely his hunger would override this ridiculous behaviour if only I would be strong enough to wait him out? But how long should I wait? An hour? A day? A week? It didn't seem wise to withhold the moderately healthy foods that he *would* eat, in the hopes that he would eat some properly healthy food. My instincts told me that it wouldn't matter how long I waited. Once William had decided against a particular food, that was it. There was no way to get him to eat it.

When William had gotten to the age of eighteen months, I had become mostly ashamed of what I considered to be his very poor diet. I had spent so much time arming myself with knowledge and good intentions but it wasn't enough. I was stumped. I couldn't understand why my investment of time and energy (meals cooked and articles read) wasn't paying off. And, of course, I was mortified by my complete and utter ineptitude. My feelings of helplessness and uselessness were overwhelming. *Why couldn't I get him to eat? What was wrong with me?*

My shame eventually turned into mild paranoia, which I tried to ignore but it wouldn't go away. I *knew* what everyone was thinking about me. I *knew* what they must be saying behind my back. I had had conversations with friends and family where we talked about other 'useless' mothers who let their children eat whatever they wanted. In the past I had been guilty of seeing and judging the lunch boxes of other children. I had silently tut-tutted over snack boxes full of highly processed 'junk'. *My* child would never be exposed to such scandalous offerings, I had said, except that now he *was* — because I just wanted him to eat! Something! *Anything!*

With each thoughtful stare and casual comment, I *knew* that they were judging me. I *knew* that they thought they could do it better. I *knew* what they were thinking: if William was their child he wouldn't be eating like that, he'd be eating 'real' food. I silently dared them to try. When their judgments scorched my conscience, I dared them to take him and try to fix his fussy eating. They thought they were so good and had all the answers? I'd like to see them put their money where their patronizing faces were... But no, probably best not.

I wondered if there was a secret ritual that would unlock William's willingness to eat. I would carefully prepare his food, and as I tentatively placed it before him and backed away, praying that he wouldn't reject my offering, I would watch to see what, if anything, would displease him this time. Afterwards I would evaluate the experience, trying to work out what I might have done 'wrong' in the past, trying to avoid repeating my mistake in the future. I was making offerings to a tiny, capricious god and I felt ridiculous. I was totally unprepared for the fact that feeding my child could be this difficult.

I had honestly thought that baby plus highchair plus appropriately sloppy and nutritious food would easily guarantee success. I *did* know that some children were inclined to be fussy; I was a bit of a fussy eater myself. What I did *not* know, and had never previously experienced, was a child who, at the mere suggestion of some pureed pumpkin, would throw a tantrum of epic proportions. Honestly! You'd think I was trying to torture him.

At around the age of three or four he started to cough and sometimes even spit if he walked past the 'wrong' food, complaining that it was getting in his mouth. We continue to discourage that behaviour, along with the screaming and running away. We have spent a lot of time coaching William to simply say, "No thank you." We are also working on his not proclaiming loudly and clearly, "That stinks!" when he finds the smells of the food around him offensive. To tell you the truth it's a bit like bashing your head against a brick wall. And, more often than not, it sounds like, "Oh for goodness sake, William. Just say 'no thank you'. Sheesh, it's not that hard." Whereupon he will usually mumble from behind his hands (which are of course protecting his mouth and nose from those offensive smells), "No, thank you."

It has been a long and frustrating journey, fraught with physical, emotional and social pitfalls. For instance, going to a Thai restaurant for a work Christmas party becomes rather awkward when you bring out a bag of Burger Rings to feed your extremely fussy eater.

It's hard for me to explain that the simple fact that William can sit in a Thai restaurant, with all those glorious smells which offend and terrify him so much, makes me incredibly proud to be his mum. Yet my pride in him doesn't cancel out my shame and defensiveness at doing something that is so totally against social conventions. I try to be inconspicuous about it. I try to do it quietly without drawing attention but people tend to notice and I politely stumble my way through those awkward moments. Sometimes I just want to scream: "I know it's not the socially correct thing to do but you don't understand what I'm dealing with!" But I don't.

Mostly William copes pretty well with going to restaurants; he almost never eats the food but he will tolerate being there without too much drama... most of the time. There was of course that time we met my husband's family for lunch at Sizzler, the memory of which is burned into my consciousness. Someone at the far end of the restaurant ordered the sizzling prawns, the sound and smell of which filled the entire restaurant. This would have been totally fine, except what do you say to a group of polite, well behaved adults when your five year old child decides to pitch a fit on the floor of Sizzler because the smell 'IS GETTING IN HIS MOUTH!'

In the beginning it was hard to deter well-meaning friends who insisted on providing food for William when we went to their house for a meal. It was hard enough telling them what William doesn't eat (practically everything). But harder still was telling them what he did eat, knowing that even if they bought the right food, he could well have changed his mind about what he liked in the two days between the explanation and the visit.

It seemed too demanding to give them explicit instructions. "Yes, he will eat flavoured rice cakes, but only this one specific variety, made by one specific company. Yes, he will eat ice-creams, but he will only eat Drumsticks, not Cornettos, even though most rational people would struggle to tell them apart."

Even water could cause problems because it tastes different in different places. William now carries a drink bottle with its own filter, but we have had to buy bottled water in some places because he just won't drink water if it tastes too different. He didn't, doesn't, can't and won't eat meat or fruit or vegetables. He doesn't eat bread or rice or pasta. And it's not just that he doesn't like them, he is totally repulsed by them and in some instances terrified. The more aromatic the food the worse his reaction is, and the more a person tries to encourage him to just try a little of something, the worse his reaction is.

Then of course, there is the problem of explaining to the other children we socialise with why William receives the 'privilege' of eating chips or rice cakes for dinner while they have to eat their meat and vegetables. I know how difficult it can be to get children to eat 'healthy' food. I respect that most of the parents and families we spend time with have invested a lot of time and energy setting standards and boundaries around which foods are appropriate for meal times and which foods are not. It has never been my intention to undermine those efforts. But I find myself stuck between a rock and a hard place. In the beginning I really struggled to find an appropriate response because I agreed with them; it wasn't 'right' and it wasn't 'fair'. Now that I understand it better myself I'm better able to explain it to children and adults.

When explaining his eating habits, I start off by saying that William's brain works a little differently from other people's. I say his brain tells him that food is scary and disgusting. Sometimes this is enough of an explanation, but sometimes it isn't. When it isn't I go a little further. I ask them what their favourite fruit is. Most kids have at least one fruit that they love and so we talk about how delicious our favourite fruits are; yummy watermelon, juicy apples, sweet strawberries. Then I tell them that William can't eat any of those things because his brain tells him that they are gross and yucky!

This usually makes kids confused. How could anybody not like *their* favourite fruit? It just doesn't make sense.

"Poor William!" they say.

"Tell me about it!" I say. If they are still interested at this point, I might go on to ask them about their favourite thing to eat for dinner. We talk about all the delicious dinner foods that we love, and then I say William can't eat those either because his brain tells him that they are yucky and gross. And they've usually got it by now; they understand (at least a little) and aren't quite so envious of William being allowed to eat potato chips or rice cakes for dinner.

My world had become very small, and trying to solve William's fussy eating had become disproportionately large. I knew that I was completely out of my depth. I didn't hide the bare facts of William's fussy eating. With all that screaming and spitting, how could I? Everyone knew about it: my husband, my mother, my family, my friends, my mother's group, and any doctors and nurses that I saw. They could see for themselves that all was not as it should be. I mightn't have had the courage to ask them directly, but I did desperately want someone to have the magic answer, to give me the piece of the puzzle that I was missing. At the same time I was ultrasensitive to any comments and every suggestion sounded like a criticism. There were a few brave souls who tried to help. They offered suggestions of strategies I could try. They tried to reassure me that he would eat when he was hungry, that he wouldn't starve himself. I was half hoping, half terrified that someone would offer to roll up their sleeves and show me how it was done. But nobody did.

I don't blame them. Even if they had been brave enough to circumvent my prickliness, they had their own lives to worry about. And anyway, I was not the only one who had never experienced such an extreme reaction from a child towards food. If there was a solution that matched the severity of William's fussy eating, I wasn't the only one who couldn't find it. At the time no one near me seemed to have it either.

In those early days, William's fussy eating felt catastrophic. I couldn't see how it would be possible for him to survive on the few foods that he actually ate. I wore myself out trying to fix William's fussy eating to no avail. There were times when I was so frustrated that I wanted to stab William's fussy eating with a sharp knife until it was a bloody, pulpy mess. There were other times when I was so embarrassed and ashamed that I wanted to crawl under a rock on a Tibetan hillside, far, far away. Mercifully, the passage of time has given me perspective. I want to reassure you that even though I haven't been successful in improving William's diet, he is still alive and growing and learning and generally being a kid. He is my gorgeous son and he holds my heart in the palms of his adorable but grubby little hands. He might not eat well, but I hope by the end of this book you will see that there is hope.

{ 2 }

where to Start?

It would probably be logical to start from the beginning, but where is that? The outward signs of William's extremely fussy eating were really only the tip of the iceberg. Like an archaeological dig: the more you dig, the more you uncover. All the little bits that I thought were disconnected were actually important pieces of a much bigger picture — like an ecosystem, with every creature relating to and impacting on every other creature.

Human beings are complex organisms. Our DNA impacts our development, which in turn impacts our behaviour, and all of it is impacted by the environment in which we grow (social, economic, geographic, etc.). It's my observation that none of it ever truly stands alone. I slowly discovered that William's fussy eating was just a part of a much bigger and messier and more complicated whole.

I tend to be a perfectionist. But my perfectionism isn't always the healthy sort that drives me to pursue excellence (although sometimes it can). More often than not it's the debilitating, life-sucking sort that stops me before I've started. That side of perfectionism sucks. I've lost count of the times that I have wished that someone else would write this story or convinced myself that I could just let it go.

But each time I thought I could just walk away, something convicted me to keep going. Something like some celebrity chef going on TV instructing other parents on how easy it is to get their kids to eat well. My initial response rages, "Really? Are you *serious*? Thanks for completely invalidating my experience and the experience of thousands of other parents!" And then once my rage has subsided I realise all over again that this project is important and I need to see it through.

I have pushed past my discomfort because I know that I'm not the only one going through this. I see you all the time, in my Facebook feed and in the comments section of mummy blogs. I know that you guys get it. I know that you'll understand when I say it's not just celebrities who remind me that I'm failing as a parent; that for every one of us there are ten, or maybe even twenty times our number of parents who actually manage to get their kids to eat well. It's hard not to find it nauseating. Just when you think it's safe to mention that your child refuses to eat meat, fruit or vegetables… BAM! There they are with their perfectly innocent and well-meaning platitudes, that never fail to make me feel like a completely rubbish parent.

How many times have I been out at a function or gathering of parents, standing around the food or by the swings, idly discussing our children, when the topic of food surfaces? How many times have I made the mistake of being honest about what William eats? How many times have those other parents just not understood the magnitude of the problem I was dealing with?

I can't blame them. If I wasn't dealing with it I wouldn't understand either and I would be that annoying parent wearing my best patronizing face. You know that face? The one that's trying really hard to show sympathy but can't quite cover up the fact that they think you're lying about how hard it is to feed your child. Yeah... *that* face.

One of the worst things about William's fussy eating was that I had become so raw, so super sensitive, that I took even the mildest of comments as criticism. How many times have I listened as they have innocently told me that their children eat everything? Or turned to their partner and asked if there is anything their little darling doesn't eat? The most innocent statements or suggestions cut me to the quick. I have listened many times as very kind and well-meaning people have offered solutions: Have I tried adding pureed vegies into his food? Or what about making a salad in the shape of a smiley face? Or cutting the sandwiches with a dinosaur biscuit cutter?

"No!" the snarky little teenager that lives in my brain declared. "Because I'm a complete moron with no brain, and no desire to help my child so I would never think to do those things. But thank you *so* much for making me feel more useless than I thought possible. Now would you please kindly go away?"

I would never actually say these things out loud. To their suggestions I would just nod and smile politely and try desperately to think of a way to change the subject. Internally I would vow once again to never,

ever mention my child's eating issues in public, then kick myself mentally, and store away the hurt in the hope that it would remind me not to do it again.

I understand that people mean well (even the celebrity chefs). I understand, but that doesn't mean it hurts me any less. I know that it's a natural response: the desire to fix problems, the urge to offer advice, to produce a magic wand and make all the yucky feelings go away. I know this because I do it myself. Isn't that at least part of why I'm writing this book? But still, it hurts. And there have been lots and lots of people along the way who have been good listeners, who have been kind and gentle, and reassured me that I'm not the worst parent in the world, despite what the horrible little voice in my head tries to make me believe.

My husband, Mike, and I both understand other people's reactions to William's eating; their doubt and confusion mirrors our own. We both grew up in working class families where money was scarce and the expectation was that you ate what you were given. Our families had similar structures, with dad working hard to earn a living and mum working hard to maintain a household and raise the kids. The food we ate was simple and nutritious. Even if some of us were inclined to be fussy eaters, the food available to us was, in most cases, nutritionally sound. We were raised in the great Aussie tradition of meat and three veg, which in my case seemed more like meat and 52 veg. We lived on meat, vegetables, fruit, bread, rice, pasta, cheese, cereal, milk and eggs. Cakes, biscuits, ice cream, Milo, and chocolate were considered to be treats. And lollies and chips were for special occasions only. It does not sit well with either of us to feed our son a diet based entirely on processed food. But neither does it sit well with us to deny him the foods, however processed, that we know he will eat.

So, you see, this is not an easy conversation to have. This is not an easy story to tell. I know that this story isn't just about William and his aversion to food any more than it's just about me as a person or as a parent. I now know that William's feeding problems weren't of my making. I know that I was ill-equipped to deal with them and that there was a mystery that needed to be solved if I was ever going to help William in the way that I longed to. I know that this mystery turned out to be not just one thing, but a massive tangle.

I'm going to ask you to understand that everything in this book is shared for two reasons. The first is to share our story. The second reason is to help you reflect on your own story, because however similar our stories are, they will not be the same. The best way for you to move forward and make decisions that suit your circumstances is to think about how what I've written applies to you. I have put in some questions at the end of the chapters to help you get started. These questions are not meant to stir up feelings of guilt or judgment, so if you start to feel guilty or judged please take a deep breath and remember that there are no right or wrong answers. You don't have to justify your actions to me or anyone else. They are simply meant to help you process your experience.

Questions

Are you parenting an extremely fussy eater?

Do you experience feelings of concern and/or embarrassment over what your child eats or doesn't eat?

Have you sought answers but somehow always feel underwhelmed by the advice you've received?

{ 3 }

Alone in a Crowd

At one point in writing this book, I asked a friend to take a look at what I had written. One of the first questions she asked me was, "Where was your family, your husband, your mother during all of this?"

Why was this book so much about me and so little about them? Weren't they as affected by William's fussy eating as I was? I had to really think about it. It wasn't that they weren't there physically, because they were. And it wasn't that they didn't care, because they very much did. I felt that I owed my friend, and you, an explanation, one that required quite a lot of thought and self-examination. I will try to explain, at least in part, why this book is so much about me and why I perhaps seem so isolated.

I am the fifth of six children. My mother is the youngest of twelve. My dad was the second youngest of four. I have over twenty first cousins. My parents loved to socialise, even though for most of my childhood we lived on a cattle property over three hundred kilometres north west of Brisbane, and around seventy kilometres to the nearest town. In between the solitude and isolation of life on a cattle property there were parties, and tennis days, and seven-a-side cricket matches, and football games, and dances, and card nights, and table tennis, and barbeques, and visits from rellies, and visits to rellies, etcetera! Life was full and round and juicy.

Our house was noisy and chaotic and I loved it and loathed it all at the same time. Too much noise and bustle had me longing for solitude but too much quiet, and I was desperate for company. In a family as big as ours, solitude was as highly valued as it was scarce. Independence was essential. If you couldn't take care of yourself you didn't survive, at least that's how it felt.

For the most part I was a quiet, contemplative and gently natured child and I guess I found that the best place to find peace, quiet, solitude and safety was in my own mind. So the more uncomfortable I felt with the chaos and disorder 'without', the further I would retreat 'within'.

I tried to run away from home once. I was protesting against the fact that everyone was being too noisy and no one would listen when I demanded silence. The demands of six year olds didn't hold much sway in the Wagner household, so in desperation I declared, "Right! That's it! I've had enough of you lot! I'm leaving!" And off I stormed. I made it as far as the second set of gate posts. They were only about 150 metres from the house and easily seen from the front patio. I guess I was put off by the seventy kilometre trek into town. I sat down in a huff expecting my mum to be desperately sad and to come chasing after me. She wasn't and she didn't. Just before dark she sent my brother up to me. I think he mumbled something like, "Mum says you'd better come home, it's nearly time for tea." So I got up and slunk home and no more was said about it. I had discovered that there was no point in running away: there was nowhere to go and nobody seemed to care anyway.

It didn't take me long to work out that being angry wasn't safe. Growing up in such a large family provides ample opportunity to become angry. I'm sure that I must have had disagreements with my sisters but it is the fights with my brother that stand out in my memories. I love my brother. We had a lot of fun growing up together, but there were times when he seemed to be spoiling for a fight. Being a girl meant that I wasn't allowed to fight. It was made clear by our mother that girls who fought were unpleasant creatures worthy only of contempt. Also, he was a lot stronger than me so the odds were not in my favour. I fought back only once that I can remember. When I did, I drew blood. Not a lot, mind you. But as the pin pricks of blood surfaced where my fingernails had left their mark, I knew in an instant that I would be in trouble. It wouldn't matter what he had done to stir my anger, to drive me to such frustration. The fault would be mine. I shouldn't have retaliated. I rarely, if ever, did so again.

When we complained to our mother about our brother, she would say, "What do you expect me to do about it?" This wasn't really a question. We weren't supposed to answer it. It was the answer to our question and it implied that we were supposed to put up with my brother's obnoxiousness; 'boys will be boys' and girls must simply learn to endure their bad behaviour. When forced to give an actual answer about my brother's bullying ways, Mum would say, "Just ignore him and he'll leave you alone." So I did my best to shut him out when he was being obnoxious. When he threatened to hurt me or put me down, I would stand as still as I could. I learned to control my facial expressions so that none of the things I was feeling showed on my face. I knew that even the minutest of flinches would give me away and that that weakness would be used against me. My fear, at the time, was very real. Now, as an adult, I can look back and see that he would never have really hurt me, but the damage has been done. Learning to speak up or defend myself instead of retreating is proving to be very challenging.

I discovered that being happy wasn't overly safe either, especially if you were *too* happy. If someone could work out what was making you so happy then they could take it away or find some other way of ruining it. When I was about five years old one of my uncles came for a visit. He had a stack of change in his suitcase, which he gave to my mum to buy something useful for us kids. Mum says he probably meant school shoes or something else equally practical, but Mum (who rarely had spare cash for frivolous treats) allowed us to choose something for ourselves. I chose a Barbie doll. For the longest time, I had thought that my mum refused to buy them for us. I mistakenly thought she was opposed to them for feminist reasons, but the truth was they were just too expensive. I guess it doesn't really matter why, because the result was the same: no

Barbies for me! I knew this was my one chance and I seized it with both hands. She was beautiful. She was a real Barbie, not one of those horrible cheap imitations. She had bendy knees and she was all mine. I loved her. I loved her so much that I couldn't wait to show her to my friends at preschool.

The only preschool in the area was in town so getting there from our isolated little farm was no mean feat. We had a long trip by car to the bus stop, and then another long trip by bus, picking up all the kids who lived on properties closer to town. The bus had school kids of all ages, including high school kids, and, in particular, one Andy Roberton. He was not a nice kid. He saw my happiness and joy and he sought to destroy it. He grabbed my prized possession, and after taunting me, he bent her leg up to her face pretending to make her pick her nose and snapped the mechanism in her knee, causing her to have a compound fracture. She was never the same again. My lesson on the dangers of being too happy was not one I would easily forget.

I am a peacemaker. I hate arguments and fighting. But just because you would never pick a fight doesn't mean that others won't bring a fight to you. I became skilled at hiding in plain sight, flying under the radar. I learnt that feelings make you vulnerable, that they are dangerous and get you into trouble. I subconsciously created a list of survival tactics. Don't ask silly questions; they only get you laughed at. Be observant. Think before you speak. Don't be pushy. Don't be selfish. Don't take up more than your share. Don't show them that you're angry. Don't show them that you're sad. Be happy, but not too happy. Feelings make you weak and will be used against you. Keep your cool and pretend not to care. It's the only way to stay safe. Be cheerful, calm, thoughtful or productive; just don't let them see how you truly feel.

I have learnt that there is a complex dance between biology and environment. Life happens to us all — the good and the bad. But each of us will respond to events in our own unique way. Some people come out swinging. I was a deer in the headlights; a turtle retreating into its shell.

This is a very small window into life for me, growing up in a big family in rural Queensland during the 1980s. It is not even close to the whole story and it would be very bad of me to leave you with the impression that I had a miserable childhood. My childhood was mostly a happy one, full of love and laughter and adventure. Not many children can watch a platypus playing in a creek from their kitchen window. Or start a bushwalking adventure by climbing over their back fence. My brother has turned into a good man, and my sisters are my best friends. My mum was and is a wonderful woman who cares about her children deeply. My dad was both goofball and hero, a giant among men (literally). I treasure the life lessons he taught me and I miss him every day. I know that my mum and dad did the absolute best they could with what they knew and the resources they had at the time.

As I said at the start of the chapter, I'm mentioning these experiences here because they have both shaped and revealed who I am and how I respond to the obstacles life throws my way and as far as William's fussy eating went, I retreated to the safety of self. It is my default state to shut people out when there is a crisis. I'm not saying that it's bad, just that it's a shame that I couldn't let those closest to me share more of the burden. In my defence though, it didn't help that we lived so far away from our families when William was little. It's a bit hard to share the burden with people who live hundreds of kilometres away. Neither did it help that the one person who was in close proximity – my husband — was our family's sole money maker, and worked upwards of fifty hours a week in a fairly high-stress job.

I often wished I could be different. I watched other parents carefully, silently searching for clues to improve my parenting. I looked at how other parents responded to their children's fussy eating and was either disconcerted by how forceful some parents could be *or* berated myself for not being like them, for not being 'better' than I was. I wished I'd known how to push for answers instead of hanging back and trying to hide just how confused I was. I wished I hadn't been so afraid. It's taken me a really long time to believe that William's fussy eating isn't the result of my deficits as a parent, but rather a complex mix of biological and behavioural factors. It's taken me a really long time to learn to ask for help and accept it. In short, I'm a work in progress.

Shannon Thiry

Questions

What was your childhood like?

Do you think your upbringing has shaped how you respond in a crisis?

What support networks (including family) do you have access to?

Do you find it easy or difficult to ask for help and press for answers?

{ 4 }

The Wonderful World of Motherhood

Mike and I had been married for a bit over a year when he applied for and was granted a transfer to a new town, even farther away from family and friends. I was halfway through a teaching degree when we moved, and luckily enough I was able to switch campuses and continue my degree. All of a sudden though, the workload had become far too difficult. I was terrified of finishing and being dumped in a classroom with twenty plus students and being expected to know how to teach. The pressure was beyond oppressive. I did the only thing that made any sense to me: I quit. I decided that having a baby would be so much easier! (And then all the parents who read this died laughing… ha ha ha ha ha… sob.)

So we 'got pregnant' and then several months later William was born, via caesarean section due to his breech position, on a beautiful Monday morning in May of 2005. It was quite surreal heading to the hospital with my pillow and an overnight bag, knowing that in a few hours I would have a baby. I had 'yikes' and 'yippee' cartwheeling through my mind the whole way in. I was so excited at the prospect of meeting my baby: a person who had never been on this planet before. I wondered what he would be like and what he would think of this crazy world we live in. Somewhere in the deepest, darkest recesses of my mind I was aware of the complications that childbirth could bring. I was just like any other pregnant woman who has the slightest interest in knowing what adventures and challenges await her — and, let's face it, most of us devour mother and baby magazines, books and/or DVDs with obsessive determination. It would be very difficult not to be secretly (or not so secretly) apprehensive about the birth. It never occurred to me, however, to be concerned about what would happen after the baby arrived.

I like to be prepared, but at times I can be stunningly naïve. It didn't occur to me that I would be anything other than completely and perfectly brilliant at being a mother. Friends who already had children tried to warn me about how hard it would be, but I, in my naïveté, thought they had become bitter and twisted. I looked at their adorable little children and I couldn't connect their words with those angelic faces. Being mother of these delightful kiddos hard? I didn't believe it! I didn't know it then, but I was about to hit an extremely steep learning curve.

You see, I had imagined this perfect life. I knew from those lovely glossy magazines exactly what a perfect mother looked like, and I was determined that I would be one of them. If there was a right way to do something (and there is always a 'right' way, right?) then that's how I would do it. I was yet to discover that children are *not* empty vessels waiting to be filled, but fully formed human beings just waiting to destroy every preconception I ever had about parenting. I was yet to discover that children have very little interest in the imaginary narratives created by their parents, or that the glossy magazines have little bearing on reality, or that my friends were neither bitter nor twisted but just incredibly tired from the gruelling and unrelenting task of raising those life-sucking little parasites... I mean delightful little darlings.

I felt slightly thwarted by my inability to earn my first set of stripes through a quick and uncomplicated 'natural' delivery. My mum had had six labours, the longest of which took somewhere around three hours. She made it seem so simple and straightforward. It just didn't enter my head that it would be any different for me. Somehow I had formed the completely unfounded idea that these sorts of things run in families. I knew it would hurt, but it was a challenge I felt ready to face. Since then I have listened to enough labour stories to be grateful that I didn't get the chance. It turned out that I have a slightly dodgy, bicornate uterus, which caused my babies to be breech. I didn't learn this until after William was born but apparently I'm quite lucky to only have a mild version.

Listening to the doctor schedule our 'elective' caesarean, I was both disappointed and a little bit scared. People kept telling me that I didn't want to have a caesarean, and giving me an alarming list of reasons why. In the end though, I wasn't given the choice and, just for the record, neither of my caesareans were awful. I was just grateful to the doctors and midwives and advancements in medical science that meant that I didn't need to risk my life or the life of my child in childbirth. So William was delivered quickly and free of drama. Not as I'd originally expected, but alive and kicking, which, I think you'll agree, is a very good thing.

Before I continue with how that steep learning curve was about to smack me in the face, I need to tell you that when William was born I fell in love, with a big fat capital L. I experienced true euphoria for the first time in my life. It was such a rush. Of course I had fallen in love with my husband, but that was different: slower and steadier. This was like being struck by lightning... BAM! I couldn't stop smiling. I wanted to pinch myself at my own good fortune. In my loved-up state, I think I even felt a bit sorry for other mothers who couldn't possibly be feeling as euphoric as I was. Michael was just as hooked. For a while I hadn't been sure how he would respond to being a dad. He just hadn't seemed that excited. But I needn't have worried because he was just as smitten as I was. Throughout all the ups and downs, highs and lows of all that would follow, that one thing, our love for our children, has remained constant.

I quickly recovered from any disappointment surrounding William's birth and was ready for the next maternal challenge: breastfeeding. This was another thing that I had planned on excelling at, only I didn't know anything about breastfeeding. Not really. I had never actually spent a lot of time around breastfeeding mothers. I just assumed that, since mothers were designed to feed their babies, it would be a fairly straightforward affair. Mother's breast plus baby equals success, right?

You might already know this, but it did not turn out to be quite that straightforward. In fact, breastfeeding can actually be quite challenging. Not only did I not know anything about the finer nuances of breastfeeding, I couldn't admit my ignorance to the midwives. Nor had I expected to feel so mortified. I didn't *want* to be prudish. I *wanted* to be grown up about it, but instead I found the whole thing excruciatingly embarrassing.

When the midwives checked on me and asked if everything was ok, I quickly nodded my head and smilingly (and falsely) reassured them that I was fine. Completely in control. Nothing to see here. My instincts, however, told me that all was not as it should be.

William slept too much. He barely cried. I couldn't get him to attach properly. Each feed seemed to last for an eternity. I'm sure it didn't help that it felt weird and embarrassing. All the same, I was quietly determined to make this work. I read every brochure and pamphlet the midwives gave me, trying to gather the information that I felt was missing. Without admitting it, or actually asking for help, I looked for the piece of the breastfeeding puzzle that was going make it all suddenly come together. I gathered pieces of information like a bowerbird.

I hadn't known that it can sometimes take a few days for the milk to come in. I hadn't known that some babies have difficulties with attachment due to the shape of their mouths or low muscle tone or the shape of the mother's nipple or a host of other reasons.

I persevered. I hadn't been able to birth him the way that I wanted to, but I was determined to do this right. The midwives gave me some nipple shields (they help to shape the nipple for feeding). They seemed to help but it was made clear that I wasn't to rely on them; they were supposed to be a short-term solution. I took their advice seriously and tried at every feed to find success without them. I had no idea what I was doing, but pretended to everyone that I did. It was a disaster waiting to happen.

I look back now and can see that this set a pattern for my parenting: knowing something was wrong, feeling lost and mortified by my lack of perfection, not asking for help, secretly gathering intelligence, trying to work it out on my own, feeling overwhelmed and unsupported and then finally feeling confused and let down that nobody could see through my bluffing to the desperation underneath. The difficulties with breastfeeding were the first of many obstacles, but how I have handled them has pretty much stayed the same.

So William slept a lot. He took forever to feed and I was never sure if he was attached properly, or if he was actually getting any milk. Still, at the end of five days I was deemed recovered enough and responsible enough to take my baby home. Even years later, when I remember all the uncertainty I feel a little nauseous.

Things changed when we got home. Everything was harder. William found his voice and boy did he use it. I was uptight and tired. All the morphine had worn off and the wound from my caesarean stung. A lot! There were too many opinions about too many things and I had nothing to anchor me. Cloth or disposable? Breast or bottle? Co-sleeping or cot? Controlled crying or demand feeding? I didn't *know*! All I knew for sure was that this beautiful bundle of joy cried a whole lot more than I had expected, and I had no way of knowing what he was crying about. If only babies were born with a dashboard and indicator lights!

I think somehow I knew that he wasn't getting enough milk, but I didn't really know what to do about it. My mum had come to help but she had to return to work after a few days. Michael had maybe two weeks of leave, but was all too soon back at work. We had been living in Gladstone for less than eighteen months. I was left alone with a brand new baby in a newish town, with no family and only a handful of newly-found friends.

I muddled along as best I could and then a day or so before William's two week check-up, I noticed something strange while I was giving him a bath. He had these raised lumps around his nipples, like little breasts. It's really hard for me to admit this but for a fleeting, ridiculous moment I actually wondered if it meant that he was some sort of half boy, half girl. Now I don't know how you react when you're scared, but I freeze. On the outside I do a fair impression of 'going through the motions', but inside it's like I've been dipped in liquid nitrogen and snap frozen.

We took him to the doctor's for his two-week check-up. I held my breath while she undressed William. Would she notice? Was she about to tell me that my baby was, as I had feared, half-boy, half-girl? But as stupid as those thoughts made me feel I was about to feel a whole lot stupider. There's no nice way to say this, so I'll just say it: I had been starving him. I felt like such an idiot. How could I not know that I'd been starving him? *Starving him?*

The doctor was quick to set us on the correct course: formula for the baby, a milk-supply-stimulating drug and a visit from a lactation consultant for me. On well-fed babies the breast tissue is covered by a nice healthy layer of fat. William had no fat, hence the raised lumps. The guilt flooded in. The only way I've ever been able to handle guilt is to expose it before it's discovered. So everywhere I went for the next few weeks I blurted out my guilt. I used to do this with William's eating as well, but I've learned that I rarely like what people have to say.

I persevered with a mix of breast milk and formula until about eight weeks before finally admitting defeat. Even on the bottle, William wasn't overly fussed on exerting himself. He would lie back with his hands above his head, as if it was all a bit too much like hard work. I thought it was kind of cute and unique. It wasn't until years later that I was able to look back and see this as possibly the first sign of what was to come. On its own it doesn't mean much, but it wasn't on its own. It was simply the first of the many little quirks that we were about to discover, which brings me nicely to the next part of the story.

Questions

What was your pregnancy like?

What was your labour like?

How did you respond to being a new mum?

Did you have any problems with breastfeeding?

How much help did you get?

Was the help you received effective and supportive?

{ 5 }

The Quirkiness Quotient

All children are different, special and unique. It's not unfair, though, to say that some children are just a bit more different, special and unique than others. Sometimes those differences are completely obvious to everyone. Sometimes they are subtle, and it can take a while for the observer to work out what the differences are.

From the outside William looked like your everyday, regular, run-of-the-mill child. But the older he got, and the more we saw him mixing with other children his age, the more we could see that he was the same… but different.

William was our first child and we loved him to bits. But that didn't stop us from noticing that he was just a little bit unusual in various ways. It wouldn't be until much later that I would be given the missing pieces of the puzzle that would allow me to see how all his quirks were parts of a big picture. But before I get to the big picture, I think it is useful for you to be introduced to William in a similar way to the way we were: one slightly confusing, often bemusing, seemingly insignificant quirk at a time.

Even though breastfeeding hadn't worked out the way that I wanted, and even though William almost never finished the recommended amount of formula, he soon caught up the weight he had lost in those first few weeks after birth. He became a much happier and chubbier version of himself. He seemed to do all the things that babies generally do. He started to smile and gurgle. I would often find him playing happily in his cot, waving his arms and 'talking' to the fairies that seemed to have taken up residence on his ceiling. One strange little thing was that he kept his hands in tight little fists and I would have to prise them open to clean out the fluff, and I really mean *prise*.

He didn't particularly love tummy time, but he did most of the normal baby things, rolling over and crawling at about the right age. One thing he had (and still has) trouble with though was sitting up. As a baby, he never looked quite comfortable in a seated position. He looked as though he might fall over sideways, frontwards or backwards. When we put him in a chair, he would sort of slump to the side, looking really uncomfortable. Wanting to save some money, we had bought a rather cheap and basic but sturdy, highchair. William would slump and look horribly uncomfortable or slide out the bottom.

Even though he was held in place only by the safety straps, we stubbornly refused to buy a new one. They cost too much and the fancier ones looked like they'd be an absolute pain to clean. I decided the problem with his chair was that the vinyl seat was too slippery and the angle of the seat was not upright enough, so being a bit crafty, I fashioned a foam wedge to go at William's back and covered it and the seat with a non-slip fabric. I look back and wonder that we weren't more concerned by William's inability to sit up. I guess we didn't want to think that there could be anything wrong with our perfect little boy.

When he was old enough for the jolly jumper, he didn't jump, but would dangle happily, spinning one way and then back the other way, quietly mesmerised. When he was old enough for a walker, he began by always going backwards. At the time I suppose I thought it was a bit odd, but it didn't seem like a big thing so I chalked it up to another one of his funny little quirks.

I come from a big family that embraces and celebrates quirkiness, so it wasn't that difficult for me to find joy in his funny little ways. His dad, having been a bit of a quirky kid as well, didn't see a reason not to enjoy William's idiosyncrasies. We loved him and enjoyed him just as he was.

When William was learning to stand, he fell as all babies do, but he didn't fall like most children, bending at the waist and landing on their bottoms. He fell like a tree being cut down—'timber!' If he was standing at the coffee table and let go he would kind of tip from his ankles and land with his head. He never actually hurt himself, but it was so bad for a while that we joked about getting him to wear a bicycle helmet, or one of those padded helmets that footballers wear. It was just another little oddity to us. I was perplexed, but I didn't really try to understand why he fell the way that he did. All the same, a little nugget of fear had begun to take root, so I started to watch him more carefully.

I wasn't a complete stranger to children with special needs. My mum was working as a Teacher's Aide in a Special Education Unit, and I had briefly studied special needs in children when I had studied teaching at university. Mum and I would often talk about what she was learning through her work. I might not have finished my degree but I was still fascinated by child psychology and early education. I was aware of Autism, ADD, and ADHD. I knew that babies could be born with vision and hearing impairments, and that any or all of these things could result in 'unexpected' behaviour in children. I quietly watched our son, but none of the things I was seeing seemed to match up with what I understood to be the signs of any of these disorders or disabilities.

So I continued to watch, and to reassure myself that William just didn't fit the criteria. I took him to all of his health checks and while the nurses were thorough and asked lots of questions, no-one seemed overly concerned. They never sat me down and said, "I'm very sorry, Mrs Thiry, but we regret to inform you that William has..." So I would tell myself that he was fine. Sure, there were quirks, but as I couldn't grasp what might be causing them I put my concerns to one side and tried to get on with being his mum.

I had thought that most babies learned to walk at about twelve months old, so it had not entered my head that William might not be walking when his sibling arrived. William was sixteen months old when his little sister Rachael was born and yet he was still not walking. So there I was with a toddler who wouldn't toddle, and a brand new baby, who was mercifully brilliant, but still hard work. Most children progress directly from crawling to walking. William, however, had quite a lengthy phase in the middle whereby he would shuffle on his knees. He was quite good at it and could easily get around, taking toys and food with him.

Hand flapping, a classic sign of Autism, appeared during the knee shuffle phase, somewhere between ten and seventeen months old. It would come out when William was very happy, excited, scared or frustrated. With this 'symptom', Autism was once again on my radar. But there were three ways that William's quirkiness definitely didn't seem to fit the Autism criteria: he was affectionate, he didn't line his toys up and he didn't hate crowds. I guess at some stage I had seen news footage or documentaries of children with Autism who hated to be touched or hugged, and who arched away from parents who tried to show their love and affection. I saw children who would obsessively line up their toys, and woe to anyone who messed them up! I also knew of children who showed extreme distress when taken to noisy supermarkets or other places that were crowded and noisy.

William loved hugs and kisses. He was perhaps a little wary of some people, but no more than a lot of children his age. Sure, he had funny little games that he would play over and over again, but they didn't seem like obsessions. One in particular involved a farmhouse set that a friend had picked up from a garage sale. It came with a tractor and trailer, a farmer and a handful of farm animals. 'Farmer Joe', as we had dubbed him, always went in the driver's seat, and the pink pig always went in the trailer, and off they'd go, in and out of the farmhouse, in and out of the lounge room. With hindsight I suppose it might seem a little bit obsessive, but he also liked to play with puzzles, books, stacking cups and all sorts of other toys.

For a short time, William went through a phase where he hated the bath. If you are a bath lover, you will know just how good it feels to slide into a warm, deep, soapy bath, and from his very first bath William had been a bath lover. When I put him in the bath it was as though he sensed he was home. He would sigh with relief and then stretch and kick lazily in blissful joy. But as he got older, moving around more and attempting to sit up, he suddenly took a very passionate dislike to the bath. He still loved water and getting wet, which made it hard for me to understand why he hated the bath so much. I puzzled over it for a bit, when it suddenly occurred to me that it might be because the bath was too slippery. I bought a non-slip mat for the bottom of the bath, and just as suddenly as he had stopped liking his bath, he loved it again.

Around about the time that he was eight or nine months old, we took a road trip from Gladstone, Queensland, where we were then living, all the way to Melbourne, Victoria, to visit my sister and her boyfriend. I think it took us four days to get there. I had started William on solid food, mostly rice cereal and some homemade fruit or vegetable purees. I knew from the glossy magazines what a perfect mother should be feeding her baby, and I tried my best to imitate that, patting myself on the back every time I got it 'right'. But taking that show on the road was going to be tricky. I had no idea how I was going to feed him while we were away from home. We got by on a combination of formula, tins and jars of baby food, teething rusks and milk arrowroot biscuits, with firm plans to return to the 'good' stuff when we returned home.

On our way home, we stopped to visit my mum and sisters in Mundubbera. While we were there, William caught a horrific tummy bug from my sister's step-granddaughter. The poor little poppet exploded like a sour milk volcano, and it didn't take long for William to follow suit. I sometimes wondered if these events (the change of menu and the tummy bug) had caused his fussy eating. Now, however, I know that even if they had contributed they were not the cause.

As a baby, William was a dream to take to the shops. Far from being upset by the crowds and noise, he seemed to hardly notice them. As he got older though, we realised that William seemed to live in a bubble; it was only when the world intruded into that bubble that he actually reacted in any way.

Shopping trips were so easy. He would sit in the trolley and babble away to me. I would often go in the early evening, after I had given him his dinner and a bath. It was beautiful and calm, probably the only period of my life in which I have enjoyed shopping for groceries! One night during one of those peaceful times at the supermarket, I ran into a mother I had first met in antenatal classes. We hadn't kept in close contact but saw each other now and again. We stopped for a bit of a chat and she commented on how placid William was.

Instantly I felt offended. I tried not to let it show but I thought to myself, "What is she trying to say? Is she saying that my son is boring?" I wasn't fully aware of it myself, but somewhere deep down I must have noticed just how placid William was compared to other babies his age. Her daughter, on the other hand, was what you'd call a livewire. (I didn't know it yet but I was soon to experience firsthand, through our daughter Rachael, the havoc such children can wreak).

I suspect that while I was feeling a little envious of her energetic and precocious little girl, she was feeling envious of my quiet, gentle, easygoing little boy. Yet her innocent compliment had triggered yet another concern. Was William too placid?

William's easygoing nature certainly stopped where food started. I have a distinct memory of trying to feed William some pumpkin puree, when he was around twelve months old. I'm sure that he had eaten it before without any problems, but this day he was not a fan. I remember him manipulating his tongue the way you might if you discovered a lump of gristle in a mouthful of food, only the pumpkin had been finely pureed, so there were no lumps. Still, William was using his tongue to find the unpleasant lump in his mouth. Then he proceeded to use his fingers to remove the finest sliver of pumpkin fibre from the tip of his tongue. He examined the offending fibre, found it not to his liking, wiped it off his finger and decided that pumpkin puree was not to his taste. He didn't gag or throw up as some children do. He simply refused to let another mouthful cross his lips. Meanwhile, mums around me at the time were feeding their children giant vats of chunky homemade purees and their babies weren't making a fuss. They loved it! All I could think was, 'What sorcery is this?' and also, 'I must never let them see just how fussy William was.'

I had been lucky enough to join a wonderful mothers' group. It started as a program run through Community Health, and continued as a regular, weekly arrangement held at one of our houses. There was only eight weeks' difference in age from the youngest baby to the oldest. We were all first-time mothers except for one, who also had a boy aged about three.

Every Wednesday I had a reason to shower and change and leave my house. I knew that I would be welcome, and that I could be myself. I could talk about the most mind-numbingly boring aspects of motherhood and it was okay because they wanted to talk about them too. No one was put off by talk of bowel movements, the colour of poo or hearing yet again how cute and adorable our kids were. We could celebrate the 'wins' of a full night's sleep, or a child's progress as they met their developmental milestones. We commiserated over what can feel like the 'brainlessness' of motherhood, and we found ways to make life a bit more interesting. We were like any group of survivors, sharing war stories, battles won and battles lost. We offered support, guidance, and encouragement and, better yet, we had morning teas full of delicious goodies.

While I didn't find our group to be competitive (as I've heard some can be), the fact that our babies were all so close in age did provide a sort of test group against which I could measure William's development and therefore (so I thought at the time) my skill as his mother. William was one of the quieter, more placid babies. He didn't seem to cry a lot and even though I felt like a walking zombie, for the most part he slept a lot better than most of the other infants.

But when they were all old enough to begin playing with each other William never really joined in. He didn't dislike their company but neither did he seek it out. He was always happy to play near them, but he didn't often play with them. It started to become obvious that his social, language, gross and fine motor development were not quite what was expected. He wasn't keeping up.

There were other difficulties, too. Toilet training was a nightmare! He just didn't seem to be able to connect that the 'wees' and 'poos' exiting his body were related to him in any way. He was never bothered by wet or soiled nappies, and was equally unaffected when I attempted to put him in training pants. He would watch the wee gushing down his legs, but seemed totally bemused by its presence and unaware of its origin. He would sit in soiled pants for ages, never complaining. If it wasn't for the smell I would never have known that he needed cleaning up.

I wondered what I was doing wrong. What was wrong with me that I couldn't get my child to learn this skill? His younger sister Rachael (who will be held back by no one) insisted on toilet training herself. She would strip off her nappy and clamber onto the toilet, never asking for my help. I noticed these vast differences in my children. They frustrated the stuffing out of me, but I was still unsure of what exactly could be 'wrong' with William. I decided that I just needed to read more parenting books, try more strategies.

You might well be wondering what most of these quirks have to do with fussy eating. The connections were certainly not obvious to me at the time. Now I can see the connections so clearly and not just in William but in other children too. It's like those wretched 3D picture books from the 1990s. You have no idea how frustrated it made me that all my friends could see the hidden image when all I could see was the pattern on the page. After hours and hours of trying to see them, it finally clicked, my eyes knew what to do and it was easy. The 3D image magically popped out and floated just off the page, and from then on I could do it any time I wanted. That's what understanding William's fussy eating has been like for me. I hope that it will be the same for you.

Questions

Is your child a 'quirky kid'?

Do they behave in ways that seem at odds with their same-age peers?

Has anyone (doctor, nurse, teacher, family member or friend) expressed concerns about your child's behaviour or development?

Are you worried about your child's behaviour or development?

Do you feel that even simple tasks are difficult to complete with your child? Getting them dressed? Bath times? Meal times? Outings?

{ 6 }

The Big Picture

"The single story creates stereotypes, and the problem with stereotypes is not that they are untrue, but that they are incomplete. They make one story become the only story." — Chimamanda Ngozi Adichie

Whenever I Googled William's symptoms (the extreme fussy eating, the delay in toilet training, his placidity and lack of interest in social play, the delays in fine and gross motor skill, and the delays in expressive language), or searched for information on Autism, which seemed the most likely culprit, I would walk away feeling confused, unconvinced and frustrated. I was confused because I couldn't find a condition that perfectly matched William's characteristics. I was unconvinced because the symptoms of Autism varied from website to website and never fully matched what I was seeing in my child. Most of all, I was frustrated because my instincts were fairly screaming at me that something was awry, but I couldn't figure out what or how or why. William's quirks had become a conundrum. An enigma. They were that funny feeling that you can't quite put your finger on.

William was eventually diagnosed with both Autism and Sensory Processing Disorder. For me, the diagnosis was bittersweet. When I read the first report that suggested William was considered to be 'on the spectrum', there they were, sweet triumph and bitter sorrow, all tangled up and confusing. It took a while for me to work out that I wasn't happy or sad. I was both. Happy to finally have the recognition we needed, but sad for what I thought it would mean for William.

There was quite a lengthy process between realising that William's quirkiness was going to cause problems for him out there in the big bad world and working out exactly what those quirks added up to. The two diagnoses were arrived at mostly within the same timeframe but through different avenues. I have separated them out, but in real life they actually overlapped each other. I will now try to give you a 'highlighted' version of these events.

Alphabet Soup

William was a few months away from turning five when he started prep (the first year of formal schooling in Queensland) and I learnt pretty quickly that when you get a telephone call from the school, it's almost never good news. Sometimes it's vomiting, sometimes it's a toileting accident, sometimes it's because your kid has taken a shovel to the head (luckily it was only plastic, but still). Even though Michael and I had our concerns about William's development and even though I was getting used to fielding phone calls from the school for a variety of reasons there was one phone call that was really hard to receive. Whilst I wasn't completely surprised to receive a call from the school's Head of Special Education Services, Keryn, it was still a really difficult phone call to take. On both ends, I'm sure. As this person I had yet to meet tried to tell me that she thought my child had ASD, my brain said 'no'. I said the word "no" to her, too.

I had already been looking, searching for a name for whatever it was that described William's not-quite-rightness. Admittedly I am not particularly good at research, but trying to navigate the world of childhood behavioural disorders is like wading through alphabet soup. So many acronyms! An additional problem is that the symptoms as listed on the internet are frustratingly vague and insufficient. When I doubted Keryn's assessment of William, I wasn't refusing to believe that something could be 'wrong' with him, at least not completely. I had read about ASD, Autism and Asperger's, and they just didn't seem (to my untrained mind) to match the behaviours I was observing in my son.

After many frustrating hours of trawling library shelves and the Internet for answers, I stumbled upon a disorder called Dyspraxia. It matched perfectly, *perfectly!* Cinderella could not have fit her glass slipper as well as Dyspraxia fit William. But was it a real disorder? Was it a medical reality or just pseudo-science? I asked a relative in the medical profession, but the question didn't fall inside the field of her practice. So I was still really confused.

There was also the question of funding. I was struggling with the idea of having my child diagnosed, but at that stage I felt that the whole point of getting a diagnosis was to get additional assistance. Without wanting to sound completely crude and mercenary, there was no money attached to a diagnosis of Dyspraxia. My instincts told me that William wouldn't experience success at school without specialist help and that more than anything forced me to consider Keryn's suggestion of ASD. Of course it's not enough for a parent to want a diagnosis for their child; there must be sufficient evidence to support a diagnosis. I did not conjure William's condition out of parental anxiety as I am sometimes tricked into thinking. William's problems are real and have been verified by several medical professionals.

Boxing

I am not much of a fighter. Those who love me most know it and have exploited it shamelessly. I often found myself fetching things for my sisters who were well able do things for themselves. They would look at me pleadingly. "Pleeeeaaase?" they would wheedle, and off I'd go, not quite sure why I was getting drinks of water or making snacks for people who were at least as capable as I was. I don't hold it against them, truly. I have to really care about something to maintain resistance or pursue an argument, and it was far easier for me to give in than to resist.

Becoming a parent has meant that I no longer have the luxury of being so amenable. I have been entrusted with the care and wellbeing of two other human lives. Sometimes that has meant standing my ground and fighting for them even when I'd really rather not. Actually... *especially* when I'd rather not.

I had heard that it was incredibly difficult to get a behavioural diagnosis, especially in regional Queensland where you might never see the same paediatrician twice (we mostly had locums that moved on after about six months). Forewarned is forearmed, so when I finally got an appointment to see the paediatrician at our local hospital, I had a plan. I had written out two densely typed pages of notes (see Appendix Two), including a brief medical history and as much as I could about William's behaviour and development.

Even with my impressive notes, the first visit was not as productive as I would have liked. I did, however, get a referral to see a child psychologist. It took a while but eventually we saw the psychologist and after we had waited and waited, and then waited some more, we finally received her report. It suggested that while William 'does not meet the full diagnostic criteria for either disorder (Asperger's Syndrome or Autistic

Spectrum Disorder)...a pervasive development disorder diagnosis is suggested'.

At the same time that I'd been waiting for this report, I'd been watching William more closely, especially at school. I realised that, as much as it might pain me to think of him as anything other than perfect, I knew that my instincts were correct. He was unlikely to experience success at school without additional assistance.

My basic expectations for my children's education were that they would be able to read, write and perform basic mathematical computations. Beyond that I hoped that they would be students who loved learning and always tried their best. Anything above that I would count as a bonus. However, I knew that even these modest expectations would be beyond William's grasp without a great deal of help. In my experience, schools are mostly unable to provide very much extra help without a specific diagnosis recognised by their governing body. As I said before, a diagnosis equals funding.

I had mixed feelings about the report, but it gave me hope. As I walked in to see the paediatrician some months after our first visit, the psychologist's report in hand, I remember seeing myself pulling on a great pair of bright red boxing gloves. This was something worth fighting for, and I wasn't leaving his office until I had what I wanted. As it turned out, it was the most one-sided fight I think I've ever had. He agreed with everything I had to say, that a child gets one shot at their early education and it should be as successful as we can possibly make it.

If I hadn't been so shocked I think I might have cried. He ticked the necessary box on the form, and that was that. William was given his first official diagnosis of Pervasive Developmental Disorder – Not Otherwise Specified, also known as PDD-NOS. This was a temporary diagnosis that allowed us to access support while we waited to see if he would grow out of his symptoms. He didn't. And about two years after that diagnosis, William was retested; the result being that he was diagnosed as having Autism.

An Elliptical Peg in a Round Hole

I am truly grateful to live in this country with access to excellent, affordable health care, but that doesn't make me immune to the frustrations of the holes and gaps in our allied health system. During the process of trying to understand exactly what it was that made William just that little bit too different to ignore, we started seeing an occupational therapist. We had initially been referred by the child health nurse to Community Health's multi-disciplinary team at his four year check-up. This meant going on the waiting list to see their occupational therapist, speech therapist and physiotherapist.

We waited and waited. We finally got to see a perfectly lovely occupational therapist. She very sweetly told us that William would absolutely benefit from occupational therapy, only to quickly inform us that she herself was soon to depart on maternity leave and had absolutely no idea if or when she would be replaced. She did give me a wad of paper full of activities and exercises that would benefit William and the phone number for a private OT (occupational therapist). That OT was no longer taking on clients (sigh) but she gave me the number for another OT, which is how we finally got around to meeting Terri.

Terri also had a very long waiting list, but we eventually got to see her and so started the process of learning what was causing William to be his quirky self. Terri didn't come out with an 'in my face' declaration of what William's problem was, but through watching the therapy sessions and listening as she explained a little at a time, I developed the confidence to keep looking for answers. I'm pretty sure it was at this point that I came across a book called *The*

Out-of-Sync Child, by Carol Stock Kranowitz. I found this book extremely helpful and I highly recommend it to anyone with a quirky kid. In it, Stock Kranowitz introduced me to a disorder that explained almost all of William's quirks and oddities: Sensory Processing Disorder or SPD for short.

Questions

Have you pursued (or considered pursuing) a diagnosis for your child?

How easy/difficult was that process?

Did/do you have reasonable access to a paediatrician?

Did/do you have reasonable access to allied health professionals such as Physiotherapists, Occupational Therapists, or Speech Language Pathologists?

{ 7 }

What is SPD?

When we were going through the diagnosis process, between 2009 and 2012, I found that Sensory Processing Disorder had not yet reached the radars of most of the health professionals I came in contact with. The Occupational Therapists knew about it, as did the Speech Language Pathologists, just not the paediatricians and GPs that I saw. Change is slow and sceptics abound but I know that SPD is real because we live with it every day. I hope that one day it will be more widely recognized but until then parents, children, and the professionals who try to treat them, must work extra hard to overcome the impacts of SPD.

So what is SPD? Well, basically it is a disorder that affects a person's ability to process sensory information. First known as Sensory Integration Dysfunction, it was 'discovered' by Dr A Jean Ayres, an Occupational Therapist and Educational Psychologist in the 1950s. Ayres developed a therapy around this idea, called Sensory Integration.

Learning about SPD helped me to imagine human beings as 'sensory processing machines' and that all humans are processing information from their senses *all* of the time. This information is not just gathered from the five senses that most people typically know (sight, hearing, touch, taste and smell), but from two more senses of which most people aren't aware. One of these senses is called *proprioception*. It relates to how we experience pressure through our muscles and joints and how they give our bodies information about how our limbs are positioned and how much force we need to use to move our bodies. The other is called the *vestibular system*, which relates to the small mechanism in our inner ear which tells us which way is up and which direction we are travelling in (kind of like our own little spirit level, but inside of our ears). It also gives us our experience of gravity, as it registers the downward pull.

As we live our daily lives, we are processing information through these senses. The information comes in and gets sent to the brain via our amazing nervous system, where our brain decides what to do with it. Not all information is important; lots of it gets filtered out. We learn to filter out most of it (the annoying hum of the neighbour's lawnmower, the aroma of a freshly fertilised lawn, the pain of the uncomfortably tight pants we mistakenly wore today), and just pay attention to the stuff that really matters (my child's scream has reached a spine tingling pitch, I really need to go to the loo, I'm standing too close to the fire). But of course we are human, which means that we are organic and therefore prone to unique construction and, unfortunately, malfunction.

Some people's sensory systems work better than others. Most people's sensory systems work fine, until they become stressed physically, mentally or emotionally. For example, I can handle lots of background noise until I've had a bad night's sleep, haven't remembered to eat or drink enough due to the hectic rush of getting kids to school on time, try to squeeze in as many chores as I possibly can while they're at school, try to remember all the things I've promised people I'd help them with, think about how on earth I'm going to fit in everything that needs to be done, and then try to cook dinner! The kitchen's still a mess because I just don't have the energy to clean it. The TV is blaring, the range hood is whirring, my husband is talking to me in one ear and the kids are screaming at each other in the background and I start to lose the plot.

I can feel my blood pressure rising and all I want to do is cover my ears to block out the noise, and assume the foetal position somewhere dark and quiet, preferably with an alcoholic beverage. This is my version of a sensory meltdown; I suspect we all have them from time to time. People with SPD experience them a lot, with far less provocation.

One of the most confusing parts of Sensory Processing Disorder is that it affects all children differently, and it affects each child differently on a moment-by-moment basis. The socks that were fine yesterday are capable of causing a major meltdown today. The too bright sunlight that sent them into a screaming fit yesterday might not be a problem today. It's possible to be over sensitive, under sensitive or sensory-seeking for any of the senses. It's possible to hate light, tickly touch but love deep pressure touch or hate high-pitched voices but not low-pitched voices. Kids can have visual processing problems but not auditory processing problems.

It's very, very complicated and hard to work out, especially if you are surrounded by unsupportive people who want to label you as a bad parent and your child as a brat. I wasn't surrounded by them, but those kinds of beliefs would cross my path and it would make me doubt myself. "Is William just a brat? Am I just a bad mother?"

Those kind of sweeping judgments have never sat well with me. The human experience is far too nuanced for me to dismiss people (myself and William included) so harshly. There is almost always more to the story, in my experience. When William was at Kindy, and I was still as confused as ever, I was very happy to stumble across a quote that seemed to sum up so well what I had been pondering for years. Why do people, especially children, behave the way they do?

> *"All behaviour is designed to meet five basic human needs: the need for love and belonging, competence and recognition, survival and safety, freedom and choice, and fun and enjoyment"* – William Glasser

What this quote said to me was that mostly when children behave badly, they are just trying to get their needs met, only they don't have the language or the social emotional skills to convert those needs into words. They throw a wobbly instead. Adults have been known to do this too. Now when I see children (including my own) throwing tantrums or having meltdowns, I wonder what need isn't being met. What exactly are they trying to communicate?

It's not possible to have all of our needs met all of the time and it's not helpful for children (or adults) to never have to wait or experience disappointment or frustration or anticipation. Yet taking a moment to ask what this person/child is trying to communicate can really help, especially with kids with Sensory Processing Disorder who often have greater difficulty communicating their needs.

A lot of the time I find myself being a bridge between William and the world. William has to learn that there are things he just isn't allowed to do. Hurting himself, others and the environment (including property) isn't okay. But I also think that it's important for the world to be accommodating of William's differences. If his differences are just a bit odd but they don't violate another person's human rights then what does it really matter? Does it matter if he doesn't wear shoes unless absolutely necessary? Does it matter if he wants to wear a jumper in summer because he likes the feeling of being wrapped up? Does it matter if he flaps his hands when he's emotional? Sure it looks a bit strange, but I love that William and kids like him challenge humanity to be more accepting, more compassionate. Just because they don't come in the standard package doesn't mean they don't have something amazing and beautiful to offer the world.

As far as I am aware SPD is something you are born with, and it is a lifelong condition. It's really important that if you have concerns about someone you know to seek professional advice. If they are displaying some of the above signs, it is possible that they might have Sensory Processing Disorder. It's also important to realise that there is nothing wrong with the senses themselves. The eyes see and the ears hear, but somewhere along the path from eye to brain and back again the information gets scrambled or misplaced and the body can respond in unusual and unexpected ways. Like screaming and running away from a banana.

Most of William's quirks relate one way or another to a malfunction of his sensory system. The clenched fists were tactile defensiveness; he didn't like the feel of certain textures so he protected himself by clenching his fists. The falling over backwards was due to a problem with processing information from his vestibular system; his body wasn't responding appropriately to the information coming from his inner ear that would have been telling him that he was falling backwards. His 'low muscle tone' which is, in part, responsible for his poor feeding and his inability to sit and his late walking, is caused by a problem with proprioception and his not registering information through his joints. He had hated the bath because the combination of issues with his proprioception and vestibular system meant he was unable to maintain a stable posture in the slippery bath. His inability to eat a normal range of foods is caused by the fact that his brain is processing smells, textures and tastes in a totally different way.

Even Dyspraxia, which matched William's 'symptoms' so well, turned out to be part of SPD. It is responsible for William's lack of co-ordination, it affects his movement and speech as his brain struggles to unscramble the messages in his brain and convert them into action. That's why his speech is sometimes hard to understand and why it takes him much longer than other children to navigate playground equipment.

Not all children who are fussy eaters will have both or either of these conditions. Not all children with Autism or with Sensory Processing Disorder will be fussy eaters. My guess, as an observer of the human condition, is that most fussy eating is caused by some level of sensory processing difficulty and that the information here will be helpful for most fussy eaters whether or not they have a diagnosis. Since fussy eating usually starts before the typical age for diagnosis, most parents of fussy eaters will be looking for help to improve their child's eating long before they consider the merits of a diagnosis.

Some people are also really sensitive to the idea of labelling children. I was for a while, then I came to realise that giving William's quirks a name didn't make them any more or less real. It just gave us an easy way to talk about them. Society is changing and becoming much more accepting of difference. More and more people are familiar with and comfortable with the idea of Autism, Asperger's and the like. We still have a long way to go, but we are making progress all the time.

It's taken a while but I've come to accept that William has both Autism and Sensory Processing Disorder. I went through the normal process of grief: denial, anger, bargaining and depression and have finally found my way to a sort of fragile acceptance. That doesn't mean that it's easy, or that I don't get sad or frustrated. I do sometimes wonder what my life (and of course his life) might have been like if William's brain wasn't so uniquely wired. It means that I've been on a great adventure and learnt a lot. He is such a beautiful kid that in a weird kind of way I think I might actually be grateful. I'm okay and William's okay, and we'll work out the rest together.

Knowing the problem was only the beginning. It didn't actually solve the problem. When you are lost it's important to *know* that you are lost, but knowing that you are lost doesn't actually help you find your way. Finding your way requires so much more, which brings me very nicely to the next part of my story.

Questions

Do you already know (or now suspect) that your child has SPD?

What are some of the ways that they experience the world in an 'atypical' way?

Are you able to see the connection between any of your child's quirks and their eating difficulties?

When your child 'behaves badly', what needs do you think they might be trying to have met?

{ 8 }

SOS

SOS is an emergency or distress signal, its meaning sometimes referred to as 'Save Our Souls'. It also stands for the Sequential Oral Sensory Approach to Feeding. This program was developed by Dr Kay Toomey and is used worldwide to treat feeding issues in infants, children, and adolescents. To me both sets of initials represent the same thing: rescue!

Earlier in this book, I used the metaphor of an archaeological dig to help you understand how we discovered William's quirks and what that eventually meant. Now I'm going to ask you to jump metaphors, from digging in the sandbox to running a race.

Before I had William, I thought that getting kids to eat would be like doing a quick, one hundred metre dash, or, at worst, a five kilometre fun run, but I have discovered that with some kids, it can be more like ten back-to-back ultra-marathons. William is one of these ultra-marathon kids, but for a really long time I didn't know that. It wasn't until I found myself lost in the wilderness that I realised we had no idea where we were or how to get to the finish line.

It wasn't that I'd gone off track on purpose, or that I didn't want to finish the race, but I wasn't racing alone. I was part of a team. My teammate happened to be a kid who, for reasons I didn't understand, screamed in terror every time I tried to get him back to the path that all the other kids seemed happy to be on. Sure there were a few kids whining about wanting to be doing something else, but they were still on the path, and they still finished the race. My kid however, had dragged me into the scrub, and I couldn't figure out why.

In the beginning I was so busy trying to be invisible, trying to hide my shame about being dragged into the wilderness by my unreasonable child, trying to hide my embarrassment at not being strong enough or smart enough to get him out of the wilderness, that I hardly noticed just how deep into the wilderness we had wandered. It wasn't until help arrived that I could finally take stock of the situation and realise what I was dealing with.

The help I received was knowledgeable, sensitive and went to the core of the problem; I finally understood what had gone wrong. I finally felt validated! There were people in the world who understood what I was talking about. They were well-educated, professional people with years of training and expertise, people I could trust when they told me that it wasn't all my fault. They gave us a rescue plan which we followed to the best of our abilities. In a perfect world we would have kept receiving their assistance until we were back on the right track, when William was able to eat a variety of delicious and nutritious food. Alas, we don't live in a perfect world and we couldn't and didn't continue with the feeding program.

For a while, I blamed this on myself. I told myself that we had become too acclimatised to our surroundings to make it on our own. It's true that we had learnt to survive in the wilderness of highly processed junk food and it had become our safe place. I'm learning that this is okay. Our lives are a journey, unique to us. We are alive and well, and muddling through the best way we know how. But the fact that we weren't able to reasonably access the extra help I knew we needed was not my fault. There just aren't enough people trained in this area of child development, certainly not in the regional and rural parts of Australia.

I knew that getting kids to eat could be a bit tricky. What I didn't realise was that you might have to *teach* kids to eat; or that some kids could actually have a completely phobic reaction to eating food. I had thought that eating was instinctive (which it appears to be for most people). I had thought that a parent's job was to provide a wide variety of nutritious and tasty food to be eaten, and that the child would mostly comply. I was so wrong! I had to learn that there are very few one-size-fits-all ways of parenting. We all exist on a kind of spectrum. The speed at which we can run, for example, varies immensely from person to person. This variation applies to most skills, including eating, which is not driven by instinct (beyond the first few months of life) but is a learned behaviour.

Some kids take to eating with gusto like ducks to water, eating just about everything in sight. These children require very little instruction or encouragement from their parents. Others eat well, but need patience and encouragement to enable them to broaden the range of foods that they will eat. Sadly for me (and possibly you) some children eat very little and need great vats of parental skill, patience and encouragement to eat enough to stay alive.

There is yet another group of children: those who do not eat at all. These children require medical intervention to keep them alive. Their refusal or inability to eat food is complete. My heart breaks for these children and especially for their parents. Their journey must be difficult indeed. I don't know much about that type of medical intervention but knowing that it exists and is available, that help is at hand should William refuse to eat absolutely everything, is beyond reassuring. As one friend has suggested, it's like having an insurance policy – you don't want to have to use it, but it's reassuring to know it's available should the need arise.

I didn't know any of this until I stumbled upon our Occupational Therapist Terri and the SOS Approach. Until then I just assumed that the horrible little voice inside my head was right—I was useless! When we first met Terri, she hadn't yet done the SOS training, but she was booked in. She gently suggested that William might be a suitable candidate once her training was completed. I was guarded and sceptical but tried to keep an open mind, and whatever she said led me to believe that it might not be the same 'shame and blame' advice that I had previously been exposed to.

In the meantime, we worked on William's low muscle tone, and gross and fine motor skills. During this time, Terri was able to move her practice from a cramped little room behind the Women's Health Centre to a much more spacious suite of rooms that she shared with a couple of Speech Language Pathologists, one of whom was also being trained in the SOS approach. By the time she was ready to start the feeding program they had quite a good set up.

When the day came to start I was more than ready. William was by then almost six years old and his condition seemed to be deteriorating. He was starting to look gaunt, his head too large for his body. When I held his hand I could feel all the little bones and tendons and it terrified me. Something had to change and soon.

Questions

How distressing is your child's level of fussy eating?
How much do their eating problems impact your day-to-day life?
Again, do you have reasonable access to an SOS-trained Occupational Therapist, Speech Language Pathologist or Dietician?
Would you have the support networks, financial resources, physical and emotional energy to pursue engagement in an SOS Feeding Program if it was available to you?

For more information about SOS Approach to Feeding Conferences, visit the SOS Approach to Feeding website.

Learning the Art of Teaching Children to Eat

Before we could start SOS, we had to go through a screening process, to make sure that William actually qualified for the program. This meant having a meeting with the dietician. For three days before the meeting I had to write down everything that William ate and drank. (The list is at the end of the chapter.)

I took the notes to the meeting. Anna, the dietician, was lovely, calm, helpful and non-judgmental. She weighed and measured William, took my notes and entered all the information into her computer. We also had to have what they call a "therapy" meal, where the Occupational Therapist and the Speech Language Pathologist performed a functional assessment of William's eating. I had a meeting with a Psych nurse, I guess to evaluate my mental health. I had expected her to remain as part of the program but I didn't see her again. I didn't think to ask why.

There were also blood tests, which were traumatic but necessary. Amazingly, to me, they came back okay. But still the overall picture that I got from all these assessments was not wonderful. William was not getting enough nutrients, not by a long shot. The dietician suggested that we should try a food supplement called Pediasure, and by some miracle William actually accepted it. I had just started making him chocolate milkshakes in the mornings, trying desperately to bump up his caloric intake, and William was enjoying them. It took a great leap of faith for me to attempt to switch out the milk for the Pediasure. If you've been in this position you know how terrifying it seems to make any changes, however small. But I did it and William didn't notice for the first few days. By the time he did I was able to reassure him that he liked it. *Phew!* Crisis averted.

After all the information had been assessed it turned out that William was most definitely eligible for the program. There was a general air of positivity that something *could* be done, that something *would* be done to help William. It was not a small commitment. Apart from the financial cost, which was mercifully mostly covered by funding we received for early intervention, we had to agree to attend twelve weekly sessions, roughly two hours each, one day a week for twelve consecutive weeks. This meant taking William out of school and committing to the homework required. Participating in the program seemed like a no-brainer, but at the same time it required careful consideration. Would we be able to uphold our end of the agreement? I thought that we could, and at the time, I participated in it as fully as I was able.

The SOS Program

This was the first time that this particular group of professionals had run this program in this format. We were all learning. They explained to me that it would be a small group program, but in the end it was just William and one other boy, who was also about six years old. For the sake of privacy I will call this boy James and his mother Megan.

We would arrive at the office, have a brief greeting, and then the kids would participate in a five to ten minute gross motor activity circuit, with lots of 'heavy' work to help regulate their sensory system. For William that meant waking him up, but for James it meant calming him down.

Next they sang a song as they marched into another room, where they were guided through a 'therapy meal'. Megan and I stayed behind with one of the team. We would quickly rearrange the room, converting it from therapy room to mini lecture theatre. There was a projector streaming video footage of our boys from the other room. This was so that we could observe the therapy meal and undergo training at the same time.

Each week the boys were kindly and compassionately desensitised to a very specific list of foods, starting with a food that they would eat, such as a plain round cracker, and working on from there. There was no judgment. The boys were not forced to do anything, just gently and patiently encouraged. There was no anger, but there was some firmness, and the boys were expected to be respectful and participate as well as they were able. I am a softy when it comes to children and I can't bear to see them being bullied, so I was very relieved to find that this program was a bully-free zone.

Each week Megan and I worked through learning of our own, with each lesson being different from the last. The first lesson was mostly taken up with sharing our journey so far. Both of us were quite wary at the beginning of that meeting. I had learned from experience to be guarded in how I talked about William's eating habits and I'm pretty sure that Megan felt the same way. It was a huge relief, though, to finally be able to open up completely and discover that there was someone else in the same boat as me. I wasn't alone any more. We shared stories and bonded over the traumas of trying to feed a child who is terrified of most foods.

Learning

The most important thing I learned from Megan was that, while our journeys were similar, they were not the same. There are so many factors that contribute to feeding problems, including how both the child and the parents respond, that no two family experiences are exactly the same.

We learnt that for children with feeding problems there can be up to thirty-two distinct steps to eating, starting with being in the same room as food and finishing with swallowing food and holding it down. We learnt that there is a developmental continuum specific to eating, starting with breast or bottle, and ending with mixed textures, and that each type of food (based on texture) needs to be introduced in order and by itself before children can cope with mixed textures.

We learnt some interesting facts about taste buds. I knew that our taste buds registered four different tastes: sweet, salty, sour and bitter. What I didn't know was that our ability to register these tastes emerges over time. I was surprised to be told that children develop the taste for bitter at around twelve to eighteen months old, the same time that William began to refuse familiar foods. We received handout after handout; each one containing detailed information on understanding the process of teaching children to eat, debunking myths and highlighting wrongly-held assumptions. I wish I could share all of them with you, but this information is best learned in the care of qualified professionals. It would be too confusing to try to make sense of it on your own.

However, I have spent most of my life living in regional and rural areas and I know how frustrating the lack of services can be. Australia is a huge country. Most of our specialist services are only available in the few major cities scattered around the coastline, and not everyone has the financial resources to get to where the help is. That's why I hope to share enough that, if you are not able to reasonably access the kind of help I'm talking about (for whatever reason), you might have the confidence to have a go yourself.

Fear is a major contributor to eating difficulties. Humans are hardwired to put safety at the top of our needs list. Any messages that our brain receives regarding hunger will be overridden by messages of fear or danger. William's instability in his highchair could quite possibly have been sending out a fear response to his brain, making it very difficult for him to focus on eating. It's important to make sure that your child feels safe and secure. If they are able to sit up independently they should have a chair with a firm base (doesn't wobble) and their feet should be on a flat firm surface. You can place a block (this could be an upturned plastic container or a safety step) under their feet if their chair is too high.

Any anger, frustration or hostility that I might have been conveying to William could certainly have been contributing to a fear response. These things on their own are not enough to cause this kind of fussy eating.

They do however form part of the picture. I wish I'd known to consider these things earlier on, to make sure that William felt safe and secure before attempting to get him to eat. I would definitely have replaced that silly highchair (which, by the way, was only silly because of William's low tone; Rachael had no problems with it).

We learnt about therapy meals and family meals, both of which had their own specific structures. Generally speaking, the therapy meals were about systematic, but playful, desensitization to food. We worked through a list of ten foods, each one relating to the last by shape, colour or texture. It always started with a blandly coloured food that both boys were happy to eat, such as a plain round cracker, and ended with a brightly coloured food that they were also happy to eat such as a lolly, followed by a drink of a similar colour; the whole time keeping in mind where they were on the 'steps to eating'.

For example, were they happy to remain at the table when slices of capsicum were placed on their plates? In the beginning William wasn't and would jump up from the table. He would try to distract whoever was with him with stories. He's a great story teller—a very *animated* story teller. I hadn't even noticed him doing it until Terri pointed it out. Once I was aware, I saw him doing it all the time. Anytime he felt uncomfortable in a situation, the stories would start. He had found an excellent way to distract me from whatever it was I was trying to get him to do.

Around half way through the twelve weeks I noticed that he was more likely to stay seated but with his body turned slightly away, still telling his fabulous stories, but now I was on to him. I have become so much better at reading his comfort levels, which really helps with pre-empting and diverting meltdowns. Before the program finished, he was actually able to touch and pick up some of the foods that had sent him dancing away from the table in the beginning. He wasn't able to eat them but it was still progress and it gave me hope.

Taking it home

Family meals were different, under the SOS program. At our usual family meal times, William would get two plates: an 'eating plate' and a 'learning plate'. The meal was to be served buffet style at the table so that all members of the family could serve themselves. On the learning plate he was to put a little bit of all the food on offer, and on his eating plate he was allowed to put only the things he wanted to eat. An epiphany! I needed to separate the act of eating from the process of learning about eating.

Family meals were not a simple thing for me. Mealtimes in our house have never been what I strongly felt they should be. In my ideal world we would be sitting down together at the dining room table to a balanced and nutritious dinner at the same time each evening. But I just couldn't seem to make that happen. My husband is a shift worker. There is no specific pattern to his shifts. His roster is random. It's difficult for him and difficult for me. The kids have never known any different pattern.

For a while I actually thought that I could be happy trying to be the 1950s style housewife, providing a balanced meal at every meal time, and keeping the house clean and tidy while Mike went out to earn the money. It was an idea that sounded fun in the beginning, but it proved to be unsustainable. I hadn't realised how much I hated housework until I had to do it all the time. I couldn't see the point in cooking just for me when he was on shift, and I quickly resented bearing the full responsibility for domestic duties.

Once kids came on the scene I was so tired and overwhelmed that meals of any sort became almost impossible. Small children have this uncanny knack for desperately needing to be picked up and cuddled at the exact time that mothers need to get jobs done, like preparing dinner. It drove me demented! So the family meals prescribed by the SOS feeding program, which should have been an extension of a practice already in place, became a major effort. I had to battle myself and my inability to find even small satisfaction in household chores. My pride insisted that I force myself to do it while we were part of the program. Having to report back to Terri, Heather and Anna each week made me accountable. But once we exited the program it was just too hard.

The progress was so painstakingly slow. I am not the sort of person who copes well with such small amounts of progress. Once the program had finished and I had struggled along on my own, the pace proved too frustrating for me. So, in weary resignation, I quit. I have given myself such a hard time over that but with the help of a skilled psychologist I'm finally making progress of my own. Not with *what* William eats, but with how I *feel* about what William eats, and how I feel about myself as his parent.

Even though, ultimately, we weren't able to master the feeding program at home, I still believe it to be an excellent program. For many reasons, it's just not accessible enough in regional Australia. It was never suggested by any of the health professionals we saw that we travel to a larger centre to access such services. I have no idea what services might be available in our larger cities. But even if it had been suggested, I really can't see us having the support or resources to make it work.

Still, I learnt a lot about eating, about William, about myself. I had the difficulties of my experience validated. It wasn't my fault that William wouldn't eat. He wasn't refusing to eat because I was a useless mother. It was the combination of his sensory issues and my inexperience and unawareness of the extent of his issues. I'm very grateful to the creator of the program, Dr Kay Toomey, and the people who helped us to implement it, Terri, Heather and Anna. Regardless of the outcome I will always be thankful for their professionalism, talent and dedication to the families they aimed to serve. Even though I didn't continue with the program, it was an invaluable experience and William did become desensitised to a wide range of foods (for a time). Even if that did not convert to his being able to eat those foods, at least he no longer ran in terror.

It's because I *couldn't* make this work that I am so passionate about sharing this experience. What might have happened if I had had the information when William was one or two, or even three years old? What if I had known not to blame myself? What if I had known how to interpret the sensory clues? What if I had known not to put such unrealistically high expectations on myself? What if parents could easily access allied health services like Occupational Therapy and Speech Therapy? A girl can only dream...

What William Ate

Friday	Saturday	Sunday
½ cup Crunchy Nut cornflakes 1 chocolate Freddo 1 Nutella sandwich (multigrain bread) 1 LCM 1 Fruit Tail 4 flavoured rice cakes 1 rice cake with peanut butter on one side and Nutella on the other side 1 chocolate ice cream 1 piece dark chocolate	Vitamin C Kids Multivitamin 1 milk arrowroot spread with 1 tsp of peanut butter ½ cup Crunchy Nut Cornflakes LCM Fruit Tail Rice crackers Potato chips 2 flavoured rice cakes Small bowl of chocolate ice cream	30 g packet of choc chip biscuits Small bowl of corn chips Vitamin C Kids Multivitamin 1 arrowroot biscuit (Attended kid's birthday party, some lollies and chips) LCM Billabong ice cream 2 flavoured rice cakes small bowl of corn chips Chocolate ice cream

Questions

Does this kind of feeding program seem like a good fit for your family?

Would you access it if there was one available in your area?

Would you be willing to travel? How far?

Would you have the financial resources, time, physical ability or emotional energy to engage in such a program?

Have you already engaged in a feeding program?

Was it a positive experience?

Were you able to maintain the program once at home?

If not what barriers to success do you think might have contributed to this?

{ 10 }

Making Connections

In April 2012, roughly a year after we had participated in the SOS feeding program, I had the opportunity to attend an introductory training course. Based on the therapy model DIR®/Floortime™, it was entitled *The Action is in the Interaction*.

I won't pretend that I came home from that two days of training and instantly implemented a course of therapy. I wanted to. I quickly learned that this was yet another task I simply could not do on my own. But, as always, I learned a lot. Even though I wasn't able to put my Super Mum cape on and save the day, I was able to take some of what I'd learnt and put it into practice, one teeny, tiny piece at a time.

DIR® is the theoretical side of the program. It stands for Development, Individual Difference and Relationships. To help children with special needs, it is important to understand that these three aspects are both separate and interconnected, like three separate cords of the one rope. Floortime™ is the therapy model that takes stock of the theory and meets the child (with their particular mix of strengths and needs) where they are currently operating. It aims to gently and playfully encourage them to progress along the developmental continuum, all the while acknowledging that every carer, parent and therapist has their own unique blend of strengths and needs that will impact on the therapy.

William is unique, his therapists are unique and I'm unique, and mixed together our approach to therapy will therefore also be unique. Wow! It seemed so simple once I heard it. It seemed that I should possibly have known this all along. But it was a totally radical concept to me. I had been trying to make us like other people, and trying to make us fit the therapy, instead of tailoring the therapy to fit us.

Three concepts in particular stand out in my memory. Firstly, I learned that child development didn't start where I thought it did, with gross and fine motor skills, language and communication skills. It turns out there is a whole other layer of child development that needs to happen before these skills can be effectively acquired. I also learned that whilst I had a pretty good understanding of William's individual differences thanks to years of occupational therapy, I had been focusing too much on where I thought he should be, not where he actually was. Thirdly, I learned the importance of understanding myself. For better or worse, I am William's mother and primary care giver. Who I am and how I respond are just as important as who William is and how he responds.

D is for Development

I had the privilege of seeing a developmental continuum or two when I was studying to be a teacher. I thought that I had a reasonable understanding of what to expect from my growing child. I was mistaken! It turns out that I knew very little about the development of tiny humans. There are many, many layers under the ones that I thought I knew about. These are sub-layers of development that are vital to social-emotional development. The first level is joint attention and regulation.

Joint attention is the ability to share our experience of an event with someone else. It looks like eye contact, and pointing, and "did you see what I just saw?" A baby looks at her parent and smiles, the parent smiles back. This is a moment of joint attention, of shared enjoyment.

Regulation is the ability to calm down after an upset, or regulate strong feelings of joy, enthusiasm, anger, etc. Regulation might start with parents and caregivers doing most of the work, giving cuddles, uttering soothing sounds, and stepping in when emotions get too big. Eventually children need to develop this ability for themselves. Of course some children develop Joint Attention and Regulation faster and more broadly than others. But they are the bedrock foundations that all other development must rest on.

Hearing this, I was caught up relating this information to my own life. What parent wouldn't eventually stop offering smiles to a baby that never smiled in return? What parent wouldn't eventually stop offering food to a child who refused to eat? I could stop feeling so guilty for not trying harder or being more persistent. I had had a natural response to William's constant rejection. Being stuck in this place of rejection and hurt feelings was awful, but now I had hope that there might be a way out. William had some competency with both joint attention and regulation, but it was fragile and inconsistent. As I tried to attend to the rest of the course, I pondered how I could find ways to build William's joint attention and regulation, to make them more robust.

I is for Individual Difference

William has Autism and Sensory Processing Disorder. Both diagnoses include a huge variation in how they are expressed by the individual. DIR® encouraged me to meet William where he was at. So instead of despairing that he couldn't ride a bike and had so far resisted all our efforts to teach him, I was to join him in the things he was already doing.

William didn't enjoy throwing and catching a ball the way I had expected him to. He would much prefer to pretend that the ball was a bomb or other weapon and that by throwing it at various objects around the yard he was actually fighting imaginary villains. So DIR® would suggest that instead of forcing him to play the way I wanted him to, I should join him in his game and find ways to build on his development. This comes more easily for some adults than others. I had quite rigid views of how to help William that looked like him doing what I wanted. It hasn't been easy to transition to a different way of thinking. I'm still working on it.

However, keeping this approach in the back of my mind has helped me to become much more relaxed. William will learn to ride a bike if and when it becomes important to him. In terms of his eating, I guess this looks like starting with the foods that he will happily eat, making sure he is getting enough 'fuel' to grow and learn and play, and introducing other foods gradually over time. At the moment we are stuck on the stage of meeting him where he is. I don't have the emotional energy, or access to the support I need, to help William progress. He appears to be getting enough nutrition to grow and learn and play, and, as much as it makes some people uncomfortable, that has become enough progress for me.

R is for Relationships

How William and I relate to each other has a huge impact on William's developmental progress. I have a host of sensory issues and personality traits that have influenced my parenting and my ability to implement the feeding program, especially once I had to continue it on my own.

When it comes to my children, I have a very low tolerance for complaining and opposition but I also don't want to crush their little spirits. So when my daughter refuses to brush her hair on the weekends, I flare my nostrils and roll my eyes and mutter, "Fine! Don't brush it then." And when William refuses to wear shoes to the shops I purse my lips, take a deep breath and mutter, "Fine! Don't wear shoes then." I can be stubborn when it suits me, but I have never been particularly good at forcing my will onto others. When William started to show opposition to the feeding program at home, it didn't take long for me to run out of resistance.

I hate waste. My time, energy and resources are precious to me and I don't appreciate having them wasted. Every meal that William rejected was an offence to me. I have discovered that not everyone is as worried by this wastage as I am, but that hasn't changed the fact that I find it intolerable. That's why I almost always offer my children food that I know they will eat. Wasting my time is just as bad. I struggled with how long mealtimes took with William. Instead of being calm and patient, I was agitated and impatient, constantly thinking of the time I was wasting and all the other chores that were waiting for my attention.

I hate food mess. When I look at it, all I can see is the time and energy that I will need to expend in order to clean it up. Playing outside in the mud with sticks and bark and goodness knows what does not produce the same effect. In fact, I love it. Inside, eating with food mess all over the child, high chair and half the kitchen? No, thank you! My dislike of housework is obviously very powerful. Unfortunately, this is the kind of attitude that can get in the way of helping a fussy eater to eat. Kids, in general, need lots of sensory stimulation. It's how they learn about the world.

This gets tricky with kids with SPD, because their sensory needs are so unique and they often strongly dislike and avoid certain sensations. It gets especially tricky if the parent or caregiver has sensory issues, too. That's why it's so important to seek help if you have concerns. It's too hard to work through all these issues on your own.

I take things literally. When my mum warned my very young self not to swim in the creek behind the house because I might die, I jumped to the very literal conclusion that the water would kill me. Not that I might drown but that the water itself was toxic. Of course the water was no more toxic than any other creek water but I didn't know that then.

So when the child health nurse told me that if I kept feeding William pureed baby food he would never learn to eat properly, I believed them and stopped giving him the puree. I later learnt that that had been a mistake, like taking away the training wheels on a bike before the child is developmentally able to ride without them. The task at hand becomes too difficult and too scary and the child simply refuses. William had needed the pureed food; it was training for the food that would follow. Taking it away simply meant that I had made it harder for him to learn to eat. The fact that he had passed the chronological age deemed appropriate to transition to more solid food was irrelevant because he hadn't passed the developmental age. In short, he had needed more time. But I didn't know that and I'm pretty sure that the nurse hadn't meant for me to take her quite so literally.

These are some, but not all, of the particular traits that stood between us and overcoming William's fussy eating. Understanding them is important, but understanding how they form part of the bigger picture is more important. William isn't growing up in a vacuum any more than I am parenting in a vacuum. It was hard for me to want to prepare meals for a child who constantly rejected them. And it was difficult for William to learn to explore and experiment with food with a mother who couldn't tolerate either the mess or waste that this necessitates, or his slow pace of learning.

What I understand DIR®/Floortime™ to say is that the key to success is seeing how all the components of this system (the threads of the cord) interact with each other, and then working with those components rather than against them. I can't change who I am, or who William is, or the developmental continuum. But I can develop an understanding of these elements and how they work in interaction with each other. I can then map a way forward. I can map a way forward by slowing down and really seeing and hearing William, working from where he is now, and gradually moving towards where he needs to end up.

The instructors of this course were also really big on learning to be playful. Whilst I don't find it difficult to be playful, I do find it difficult to force playfulness. I am not Mary Poppins. A spoonful of sugar does not help the medicine go down. When there's hard work to be done you just roll up your sleeves and get on with it. Work is work and play is play. This is true when the work is particularly unpleasant, like feeding children who don't want to eat.

I really haven't progressed much with this principle. I don't have the emotional energy to turn his fussy eating into a game, but it would seem that this is a major contributor to success so it is worth some thought. How could you incorporate a more playful attitude in your interactions?

The instructors suggested less talking and more watching, more following and copying, and joining in with what the child is doing. They suggested more 'ooh-ing' and 'aah-ing', using sounds instead of words (especially with non-verbal children). They also introduced me to the term 'playful obstruction'. I already did it; I just didn't know it had a fancy name. It means pretending not to understand what your child wants. So when they point to a toy or a food and indicate through noise that they would like that object, you pretend they want something else. So if they point to the boat you reach for the ball and say, "Oh you want the ball." And when they get frustrated because you got it wrong you do it again (but not so much that you really upset them—be a little bit sensitive). Of course you end up giving them what they want, and as you give it to them you tell them, "Oh, you wanted the boat! Silly me." The feeding program also called for a level of playfulness that I just wasn't able to sustain.

There is so much more to DIR®/Floortime™ than my limited understanding; and so many other valuable and important therapy models of which I have little or no knowledge. The important thing to me was not the particular therapy model, but the fact of learning, of understanding the intricacies of our particular circumstances, and of getting the help and support that we need.

Questions

Does your child have any issues with joint attention and regulation?

Are they able to engage with people and events?

Do they point? Do they ask questions?

Do they seem to get upset frequently or without much provocation?

Are they able to calm themselves?

Do you find it difficult to engage with your child?

Are you able to examine your parenting style without judgment and see where you might be hindering your child's progress rather than helping it?

Do you have any sensory issues that might be getting in the way?

11

Recognising Grief

grief (gri:f) n **1** deep or intense sorrow or distress, esp. at the death of someone. **2** something that causes keen distress or suffering. *Collins English Dictionary*

When I was twenty one, my dad died. It was cancer, and he was fifty seven years old. I couldn't believe that it was real so my brain concocted a fiction to help me get through. The fiction was this: *my dad's death wasn't real*. It was a test. The 'universe' wanted to know what I was made of. Could I grieve well? Could

I grieve politely, with dignity? If I could, then I would be rewarded and my dad would be returned to me and all would be well. So I rose to the challenge and I grieved with dignity and grace. I held my head up. I wept silently. I accepted condolences with equanimity. I did everything 'right'.

Sometime after the funeral I had a dream. In the dream my dad's death was just a practical joke. A very lame and extremely unfunny practical joke. My dad and some of his mates had pulled the mother of all pranks on us, and as they all tumbled out of the car (my granddad's white and gold Holden Kingswood), laughing and congratulating themselves on our stunned and stupefied faces, I was so relieved. Angry, but relieved. I couldn't believe they had put us through all of that for a stupid joke.

But then of course I woke up and it wasn't just a joke, and my 'perfect' grieving hadn't been rewarded. My dad was dead. Never again would I be wrapped up in one of his bear hugs. Never again would I see his bright blue eyes twinkle and his face crack open with his lopsided grin. My life would never be the same. His death had ripped a hole in the space-time continuum of my life. The hole is still there, its edges flapping in the breeze. It has not healed up. No one has plastered over it. It has become part of the furniture of my life and as such I don't always see it. But every now and again something will happen and I trip over it and I remember. My dad is dead. And I can't breathe because of the pain in my heart.

I know what grief is.

I thought I knew all there was to know about grief. But then I had William.

I love William with all of my heart, so how could I possibly feel grief over this gorgeous, blond haired, greeny-blue eyed bundle of enthusiasm? It seems impossible. It's so implausible that it took me quite a long time and many doctors, psychologists, books, and hours of daytime television to expose this hidden truth.

When the kids were little I was angry almost all of the time. I thought it was because Mike almost never helped in the kitchen, but it turns out it was a little bit more complicated than that. I eventually realised that part of my anger was due to my perfectionism and anxiety, but a lot of my anger was due to grief. I had mistakenly thought that grief was something you only experienced when somebody died, or was horribly wounded, or when you lost everything you had in a house fire or an earthquake. It didn't seem possible that I could be grieving when I had everything I thought I wanted. Yet somehow or other along the way, I discovered that I was grieving. I was grieving the loss of a dream.

I used to watch a lot of daytime television. It seemed to go with the territory, stuck at home with two young children. On one of those seemingly endless days, I saw an actress being interviewed about her divorce. She commented on her grief and how it was accepted that a person would be grieved when a spouse died but not necessarily over a divorce. She felt that there was an expectation amongst her friends that instead of grieving she should be celebrating. For her, the pain of that loss, though less expected, was every bit as real. She had had to give herself permission to grieve.

Her words struck a chord and I realised that I was grieving what I had 'thought' motherhood and parenting was supposed to look like. William's Autism and Sensory Processing Disorder have altered the course that we *thought* we were taking. And it doesn't just affect me! It affects us all; me, Mike, William, Rachael, grandparents, aunts and uncles, cousins and friends. All of us had dreams and expectations about what life was going to be like with William in it.

It's such a huge part of what makes us human, this ability to plan and to dream. And the world encourages us to dream big. But I reckon it also encourages us to dream small. Perfect little lives, with everything neat and tidy and all stitched up. Before William's Autism and SPD became apparent, I had this whole other life mapped out for us. But like the proverbial missed ship, I have had to stand on the docks of the life I've been given and watch my perfect little dreams sail away on the tide. It doesn't matter how much I stomp my feet, or shake my fists and yell that it's not fair. Life goes on. There are groceries to be bought, meals to be prepared, dishes to be washed, meltdowns to be negotiated (mostly mine). There is no time to stand around moping. But somewhere between saying goodbye to that perfect little dream and moving on with life, I realised that I had to make room to grieve. Disappointment would let bitterness overwhelm me. Acceptance would set me free.

So I gave myself permission to grieve. I gave myself permission to be pissed off. I gave myself permission to let go of that perfect little dream. I had a choice to make: I could stand on the docks pining for my lost dreams or I could make the most of my gloriously imperfect reality. I won't pretend that it has always been easy. It's very hard not to be angry when William has soiled himself for the fifth time that day and it's not even lunch time. Or when he is stuck on a thought or idea and won't be swayed or diverted. Or when he comes home from school and is completely devastated because someone has been mean to him when he tries his very best to be kind and thoughtful to everyone.

It's hard not to be angry when someone has inadvertently or overtly expressed the opinion that I do too much for William, or they imply that he'll never learn to be independent if I keep coddling him. They don't see that when I push him to be more independent, he dissolves into a puddle of tears and frustration or total and infuriating belligerence.

William gives new meaning to the term 'stubborn as a mule'. They don't know how much he has improved, how much progress we have made. I see families with kids his age who appear to be living life easily while we struggle with the mundane and it hurts.

Like my dad's death, William's Autism and SPD have also punched a hole in the fabric of my life. Unlike my dad's death, I haven't actually lost William in a physical sense, just the dream version of him. The dream I had of my child, of the kind of mother I thought I would be, of the kind of life I thought we would have… it was only ever a fantasy (and not even a particularly good fantasy).

I was in a dangerous place. I might have spent a lifetime pining for a different William and a different life and being angry with the life I have been given. I'm so glad to have been pulled back from the edge of that disaster. Because the truth is that I don't have room in my heart to love the real-life, flesh and blood William and at the same time pine for that weak, watered-down dream version. I'm so glad that my heart has chosen love. The actual, real-life William is awesome and amazing and it turns out that I love him just exactly the way he is.

This doesn't mean that I don't believe in therapy (early intervention is beyond awesome) or helping William to achieve developmental goals. It means that I don't feel like I have to 'fix' William anymore but rather to help him become the best version of himself: his true self, not that weak imitation that I had conjured up. I no longer feel as though I have failed when a therapy proves just too difficult for us, when the cost, or travel distance, or time, or emotional energy required is just too great. I am able to just let it go, knowing that if it's really important we will eventually find a way.

One night, when he was about nine or ten years old, as I was putting him to bed and kissing him goodnight he looked at me with this odd look on his face. It was smugness, trying very hard not to be. He was happy about something but was aware that it wasn't nice to be too proud of his good fortune. Anyway, he looked at me with this look on his face and said, "I really have a perfect life." And my heart melted. All the challenges we have faced and all the ones we can only imagine flashed before my eyes. Then just as quickly I saw all the great things about his life. A safe and comfortable home to live in. Food to eat. Clothes to wear. Endless hours of superhero shows to watch. A family that loves and accepts him just the way he is. And I said, "You know what, Bud? I think you might be right."

"You can't control the wind, but you can adjust your sails." German Proverb

Questions

Has reading this triggered any unresolved grief in your own life?

Have you allowed yourself the time and space to grieve?

Have you considered seeing a professional such as a Psychologist or Grief Counsellor to help you process your grief?

Can you see past the hurt of living a life you didn't choose, to the treasures that lie in the life you have?

12

The Importance of [M]ental Hygiene

I may have mentioned a few times that I have struggled with perfectionism, anxiety and depression. It recently occurred to me that taking care of my mental health is a lot like taking care of my dental hygiene (hence [m]ental hygiene, geddit?). I need the right tools. I need to act daily, and it helps to see a professional on a regular basis. And when that shooting pain starts, I had better ring up and make that appointment.

I have thought nothing of going to the dentist. It seems like a sensible thing to do, and it is an investment in one of my greatest assets (everyone wants a nice set of chompers, don't they?). Yet, I was reluctant to see a counsellor or psychologist, even though I knew I was in a great deal of emotional pain. It wasn't that I didn't value my mental health; it just somehow seemed like an admission of defeat. Somehow I was supposed to know how to work through these things on my own.

I also had this misconception that there was something self-indulgent about paying someone to listen to my problems. Farming folk tend to be rather stoic (and stingy) creatures, especially when it comes to all that ooey-gooey, emotional stuff. And, despite the fact that I barely know one end of a cow from the other, I am still a farmer's daughter. We aren't meant to talk about our feelings. We just bottle them up, starve them of oxygen and hope like hell that they'll shrivel up and die. Only, for me, it wasn't working very well. My feelings kept leaking out, sometimes as tears, sometimes as white-hot, blinding rage.

In 2013 we moved again, this time with children, who were very unhappy at having to leave behind everything they had ever known. We didn't move that far, only about 330 kilometres south, but it was far enough to make visiting old friends an inconvenience. Mike seemed blissfully unaware of the trauma the move had caused or the fact that I wasn't coping at all. I decided that I needed some extra help.

A new friend, who had also had some mental health struggles, gave me the phone number for her psychologist. Karren (the psychologist) quickly corrected all my unhelpful beliefs about seeing someone, simply by asking if I could hear how hard I was on myself. I hadn't realised that I was being hard on myself, but maybe it was a little unfair to say that seeking help for my happiness and peace of mind was self-indulgent. So I began to go without the guilt. I went, and I still go now because I needed the help of a skilled professional to manage the leaking of tears and white hot rage.

Karren has helped me to see that the perfectionist in me is not easily satisfied. Her standards are impossibly high (the perfectionist's, not Karren's). And she (still the perfectionist) is unafraid to chastise me when I fall short, which of course is all the time. And so I give up. Why bother trying to please such an unreasonable creature? Nothing I do is ever good enough. But then she gets under my skin and points out that "other women" are capable of reaching her standards. She is very convincing and so I envy women who seem to me to have it 'all': a helpful husband, a clean and tidy home, obedient kids and a challenging and rewarding career. I look through the store front of their lives and I want what they've got. I start to think that I can do it, I can have what they have, but fear of failure stops me. There is no point in even trying because I will never be as good as those other mothers. I cannot enter their glossy, perfect lives no matter how much I press my nose up against the glass.

So I become angry with my husband and children instead. Only I can't yell and get all that pent-up aggression out. I have to squeeze it out in a series of passive aggressive tantrums, stomping down hallways and closing doors with more force than is necessary and muttering swear words under my breath. And in my head is a constant stream of poisonous, toxic thoughts. I become convinced that Mike and the kids are standing between me and my plans for ultimate perfection.

After the anger burns itself out, the guilt floods in. What kind of monster am I? My husband and my children are wonderful people. Mike works really hard to provide for us all, and the kids are, well… kids. None of them cares about my perfectionist agenda. They are all happy being themselves, and very busy not caring that I'm not perfect. If there is something to be learned from them I'm not quite ready to concede to it yet.

Karren calls this part of my personality 'Miss Perfect'. It is Miss Perfect that likes to tell me that I'm not a good mother. And the tiny grain of truth in it hurts. I know I'm not awful. I'm not Joan Crawford or anything. I love my kids and they are mostly well looked after, so long as you don't look too closely. If you don't examine our dining habits, or our personal hygiene habits, I'm probably doing okay. Please don't ask me when was the last time I cleaned the bathrooms, or vacuumed and mopped the floors or, for heaven's sake, washed the sheets. Tabloid TV could do an exposé on how often my kids *don't* clean their teeth. My mum would be horrified.

The point is, Miss Perfect is there to remind me of all my mistakes and how other mothers are doing so much better than I am. How she knows this is something I'm learning to question. I don't have to dismiss everything she says. Sometimes she has something valid and useful to say. But now, instead of believing every vile and critical thought that pops into my head, I am learning to be discerning. I can hold on to the thoughts that are helpful and try to reject those other, less helpful thoughts.

I feel like it's taken me forever to get here, to get to this place where I know who I am and what I'm dealing with. Perfectionism, anxiety and depression... they're like a trifecta of emotional tyranny. Like William's issues with Autism and Sensory Processing Disorder, perfectionism, anxiety and depression are not one-size-fits-all. They do not always look the way we have been led to believe, which can make them really difficult to recognise, especially in ourselves.

One of my first wake-up calls happened when I was in my GP's office. I don't remember what I was there for, but somehow or other the topic turned to my anger issues. My GP asked me if I had considered that my anger might be anxiety coming out sideways (probably not her exact words, but close enough). *Hmmm... interesting*, I thought. I'm fairly calm. I go with the flow. I didn't have any phobias that I knew of. Yet, the doctor's words brought all kinds of memories swimming to the surface, memories of being angry and uptight for no good reason. Could that anger have been caused by anxiety? I hadn't considered myself to be an anxious person, but maybe it was worth giving it some thought.

Around the same time, the kids and I visited the local duck ponds with my mothers' group friends. As we took a walk around the edge of the pond, I warned my kids not to fall in because I couldn't promise that I would rescue them; that water was putrid and I really wasn't sure that I would be able to go in after them. To make things worse, the group decided to stop on some rocks to attempt to catch some tadpoles.

I couldn't join in.

I let my kids join in because, philosophically, I think it's important for them to enjoy these experiences. But I stood frozen on more stable ground, while they all jumped from rock to rock, leaning over the water eagerly. The whole time I was terrified and angry. What kind of stupid, reckless person encourages their children to engage in such dangerous behaviour? Why did all the other mothers look like they were having a great time? All I could see were the terrible things that could go wrong. Kids falling and smashing heads on sharp jagged rocks before disappearing into that murky water. Yuck!

I hated that I couldn't just enjoy the moment. I was feeling uptight and angry. I really just wanted to snatch the kids up and escape. Was this what it meant to have 'anxiety'? I waited until I could bear it no longer. I gave my kids their 'five minute' warning and then we left. As I drove away from the duck ponds that afternoon, with tears of confusion (why was I reacting like this?) and relief (my children survived!) pouring down my face, I considered my doctor's words again. Maybe I was a little more anxious than was strictly necessary.

Depression is my other nemesis. I can be travelling along quite nicely, thinking that I've got this whole life thing sorted, when, all of a sudden, depression will knock me down. Like an earthquake, hidden and rising up from the deepest depths, depression is something that happens *to* me. I don't create it and I can't stop it. I just have to learn to survive it. I can learn to look out for the early warning signs. I can batten down the hatches and have my emergency kit ready, but how frequently, and how long and how strong the tremors are, is out of my hands. That's how I see it anyway. I feel lucky that my depression is not very severe, and that I'm making great progress thanks to Karren's expert assistance.

There really is something about having a plan of action, about being prepared that eases the fear and panic. Again, this has taken a while. Those wretched stereotypes had raised their deceptive little heads once more. I didn't think I was depressed because I could get out of bed in the morning and I wasn't crying all the time. Isn't that what depression is supposed to look like, like someone with greasy hair and red-rimmed eyes, wearing stained pyjamas? When doctors and nurses asked if I was 'coping' I said yes, because I thought I was. But what does that even mean? Coping?

I was tired. So very, very tired. And I was angry almost all of the time. I didn't want my husband breathing the same air as me, stealing *my* oxygen! The kids needed more from me than I was happy to give. I was dragging myself through the days, but I hadn't run away or hurt anyone. The house was a mess but I always managed to have clean dishes to eat from and clean clothes to wear. Was that what coping looked like? Because if so, I was coping like a champion! And, you know, sometimes I was actually happy, laughing and smiling and enjoying life. Sometimes I actually liked Mike enough to let him breathe the same air as me. I cleaned the house and cooked healthy meals. I played with the kids. Then there were those scary times when I wanted it to all be over, or rather, to never have begun. Those times woke me up to the fact that I wasn't 'coping' at all.

I needed some help. I was afraid of those thoughts. I hated how they made me feel. First, the trapped and suffocating feelings would arrive. I would strategize my escape. Thoughts of suicide would usually crop up — it is after all the ultimate escape. But then, suicide never ends well, so maybe a job would help. Oh, or a divorce, yes, definitely a divorce. Only I had no money and the rational part of my brain was loud enough to remind me that Mike wasn't really the problem (actually he's pretty nice but *shhh*, we don't want him knowing that). I didn't really want a divorce. And then the embarrassment of being a grown woman who throws tantrums would come and there was no way I could apologise (I think they call that pride). And after I had broken Mike's spirit and my anger was burnt away, I would finally relent, and that's when the guilt of ingratitude and entitlement would come. I had the privilege of being white, financially stable and living in one of the safest and wealthiest countries on the planet. How dared I claim that my life was difficult? How dared I claim to be depressed when I had everything? Everything!

I don't understand depression. Not really. But I understand that for me it's a warning sign that something in my life is out of balance. So now, instead of blanking out those scary suicidal thoughts, I try to sit with them and figure out what part of my life is out of kilter. I also have Lifeline on speed dial, just in case. And if things get bad, I know to ask for help. Getting out of the house and talking with friends and family really helps. A problem shared is a problem halved and all that.

Raising children is a nerve-wracking business. Talk about an emotional roller coaster! Sometimes it's up and it's awesome, like swimming with dolphins. Other times it's down, *way* down and then it's a bit like being eaten alive by piranhas, one teeny-tiny, savage little mouthful at a time. And in the middle is the grind, the everyday, the hard slog. I really don't want to sound ungrateful but there are definitely times when I am frustrated by the mindlessness, the monotony, the 'groundhog day' of it all. I can't help but wonder: what am I actually contributing to society?

That's why I now think it's so important to work at good mental hygiene (health) practices, to do the daily things that are going to help keep the decay away. I don't need to wait for someone else to validate my existence. I am awesome. I am creative and kind and loving. I am raising awesome kids. Being a stay at home mum *is* a valid contribution to society. Not more or less valid than other contributions. This is not a competition, this is just life: messy, complicated, glorious life. There is room for all of us.

No, I don't practice perfect mental hygiene, but I am trying, and slowly but surely I am making progress. The journey of a thousand miles begins with a single step. How do you eat an elephant? One bite at a time! How can I be truly kind to others if I am not first kind to myself? How can I raise children who will be kind to themselves and others if I do not show them by my own example? That means being open and honest. It means showing up every day and dealing with whatever gets thrown my way, even if showing up looks like yesterday's clothes and six cups of coffee and even if 'dealing' looks like the absolute bare minimum of surviving the day. It means setting a good example by showing that I am vulnerable too. And showing that I make mistakes, I get it wrong and that's okay.

I don't just want to be good for my kids or my husband; I want to be good for me. Because as hard as it might be for them to live with a woman as emotionally 'messy' as I am, it is even more torturous for me. After all, they can escape me, but how can I escape myself? Much better to work on a 'self' that I don't need to escape from. Also, to bring it back to helping William with his fussy eating, I feel that by taking care of my own mental health I'll be in a much better position to help him with his eating and with everything else. Well, that's the plan, anyway.

Questions

How's your mental hygiene?

Are you tired of being tired?

Are you often angry without a good reason?

Do you feel overwhelmed by your responsibilities?

Do you feel alone or unsupported?

Have you seen or would you considering seeing your GP for a referral? (NB: One GP that I asked for a referral suggested that I didn't really need one as I 'looked' like I was okay. Do not accept that. Let's pretend for a moment that setting the standard for our mental wellness a little higher than acceptable personal hygiene is okay. Okay?)

{ 13 }

Finding Faith

I have spent most of my life believing that there was not much need for faith. After all, we live in a modern world of logic and science. Mythology, religion, creation stories and personal faith were interesting to me as curiosities of human nature. I was very magnanimous about it. Each to their own, I would say. But as far as I was concerned, people who believed in spiritual things were — honestly? Well, I thought that they were a little bit weird!

But it seems that I have had a change of heart and although it might not appear to have an obvious link to William's fussy eating, it was William's fussy eating (at least in part) that led me to my change of heart. And it is this change of heart that has helped me cope with William's fussy eating with so much more grace.

Before I continue, I want to say that I know the issue of faith is sensitive and emotionally charged for many people. I want to state quite clearly that I am no more an expert on faith than I am on Autism, or Sensory Processing Disorder, or anxiety, or depression. It is not my intention to pretend to be. All I'm trying to do is share my experience as honestly as I can. If you have strong feelings against religion, if reading this chapter is likely to cause you distress, then please skip it. I respect that many people have been deeply wounded by those who have professed to have faith and so I have tried to keep all material of a religious nature contained to this chapter. This is, after all, a book about fussy eating, not about faith. I would hate for anyone to feel ambushed or manipulated. If you are going to skip this chapter, now is a good time to do so. Otherwise please carry on.

I was raised in a loving, but non-religious family. Faith was not something I spent a lot of time thinking about. We kind of free-wheeled through life, accepting a person's right to choose for themselves, but not really identifying with any particular religion or belief system. In the days when more people went to church than didn't, my dad's family (being German) were

'Lutheran' and my mum's family (being obstreperous[1]) were 'Protestant'. Which somehow or other made us 'Uniting' even though we never went to church and didn't profess to believe in God. We were raised to be honest, kind and thoughtful, which seemed enough at the time. I was fairly convinced that there was no God, and as I got older, I identified as being an atheist. I had a vague, intellectual curiosity surrounding religion, but no real desire to find out more.

On the surface my life was pretty good: a happy childhood, a decent education, married to a good man and mother to two delightful, if somewhat exhausting, children. Other than the death of my father (lovely, lovely man) when I was twenty one, I had experienced very little in the way of pain or suffering. I was a fairly happy person, almost bubbly. People often complimented me on my smile, and they seemed to like me, even though I was never quite sure why.

Underneath that happy, smiley exterior was a brain that never stopped thinking. Mostly my thoughts were contemplative, wondering about the world and the people in it, but sometimes, usually under stress, my thoughts would turn to darkness. I don't know why I

---

[1] Obstreperous means "noisy and somewhat uncontrollable", and that was a joke (in case you missed it).

felt such darkness. All I can tell you is that for most of my life there was this shadow of doubt, lurking, poking. I felt loved as part of the family unit, but sometimes I also felt that I was a burden, another mouth to feed, another child making stupid mistakes and asking stupid questions. Even as young as six, I had started to wonder if my family might not be better off without me. That is really hard to admit. There's no one to blame for my feeling this way. It was just... there. It wasn't *always* there. Most of the time, I was too busy being a kid and having fun. My guess is it would appear when I was upset with myself or in trouble with someone else.

As I got older, I marvelled with wonder at the vastness of the universe but I could see humanity stretching out into the past and the future and it just seemed so pointless! Thousands of generations of humanity living lives on a teeny-tiny planet suspended in endless space. Why? To what end? Could there even be a point to something so eternally monotonous?

Then, one day, I was the mother of two beautiful little people. I had been charged with a very great responsibility and I was failing. As I was standing in my cluttered, messy lounge room, I was completely overwhelmed with the hopelessness of my existence.

It wasn't the first time this darkness had bubbled up, but this time was the worst. In my imagination I saw a big black hole opening at my feet and I wanted with every fibre of my being to fall in, not to die (because I didn't want to cause pain to those that I loved), but to never have existed. I wanted to be completely erased from time and space. Why did I have to live with the pain of always knowing that I would never be quite good enough, somehow always lacking, always failing?

Why did I have to endure the pain of failing at being a good enough daughter, a good enough student, a good enough friend, a good enough wife, and, worst of all, a good enough mother? I didn't want to kill myself and cause my children that kind of pain but I knew that for me to live, there had to be more! There had to be more than cells, more than DNA, more than dirty dishes and what often felt like the never-ending drudgery of being a wife and mother.

I had scared myself and so I went to a psychologist for a while (this was in Gladstone long before I met Karren) which seemed to help. But I still couldn't shake the feeling that there had to be more. So I started looking for answers. My mind, which had been closed to all things spiritual, slowly began to open. I read books on Buddhism. I explored New Ageism and I learned how to perform Reiki, which opened my mind to the idea that maybe, just maybe, there was a God or higher power, or intelligent energy that connects and spurs life onwards.

I did not plan on investigating Christianity. From my very limited experience and what I could gather from TV and various other sources I had decided that Christians were, generally speaking, not very nice people. The list of their offences was quite long: hypocrisy, self-righteousness, greed, abuse of power, sexual abuse, and many, many more besides. It's true that some people who have called themselves Christians have committed some of the worst crimes in human history. But does that mean that all people who call themselves Christians should be guilty by association? I didn't even realise how prejudiced I was until I had a reason to challenge those convictions.

Enter stage left: a friend and Christian, Kylie, an intelligent and articulate woman whose integrity I admired. We had met not long after our oldest children were born. We were in the same mother's group. I knew she was a Christian but don't ask me how I knew because I don't remember her talking about it. A couple of years later, she and her husband and their two boys left for Nepal for two years. They went to teach and to work for an NGO providing support to some of the poorest and most disadvantaged people of Nepal, which impressed me greatly. I knew that Kylie had a passion for helping the poor, and here she was, not just talking about it but doing something about it, not that you have to be a Christian to do that, but still... When they returned to Australia, our oldest kids were at school together and our next oldest kids were at Kindy together. We began to run into each other a fair bit.

I wasn't in a very good place, mentally speaking. I was having what I like to call my 'existentialist crisis', and kept throwing out flippant comments about the pointlessness of life, and about humanity being a plague on Earth. And she would respond in ways that surprised me, intrigued me. We talked about other things too. It was nice to talk to someone who was interested in deep and thought-provoking topics. I was challenged by her, which (without meaning to sound conceited) doesn't happen that often. Not only did she seem to have her life under control, but her opinions were considered and well-informed. She cared deeply about big important issues, like human trafficking, fair trade, and global warming.

After to-ing and fro-ing, and skirting around the subject, Kylie was brave enough to loan me a book called *The Jesus I Never Knew* by Philip Yancey (I still have the note that she had slipped inside the front cover; I will treasure it always). The Jesus he talked about was certainly a great man. I started to read the bible to verify Yancey's claims and I met the most amazing man, a man who stood for truth, justice, kindness, mercy and love. A man who hated hypocrites, who declared woe to the religious leaders who burdened their followers with rules and regulations that they themselves refused to keep (check out Matthew, chapter 23 if you are interested). I didn't agree with everything I read in Yancey's book, but I remember saying to one of my sisters that, even though I doubted I would ever call myself a Christian, there was something special about Jesus.

So began a hunger to learn more about this Jesus character. More reading, a few DVDs, more discussions with Kylie and my doubts and objections began melting away. I want to be clear that, while Kylie was receptive to my curiosity, she was never pushy; I knew that I was free to disagree and that if I stopped being interested then she would have accepted my decision and our friendship would have continued just as it had before. But I didn't stop being curious. I wanted to know more.

Kylie had loaned me a DVD series called Alpha. It's a basic but thorough introduction to Christianity. The kids were at school and Mike was at work, and I was sitting in our lounge room in front of the TV trying to pay attention to it all when I suddenly thought, 'Well, if there is a God, and he is good, then where has he been? Why do I feel so utterly alone?' I closed my eyes and I felt this inexplicable presence. I was overwhelmed with the sense that I had never been alone, but that I had been held in the palms of some very big, loving and gentle hands. And, whoever had been holding me, had been waiting patiently for me to feel his presence. It sounds strange and weird, but that's the truth. It was a beautiful feeling and I wanted more.

Eventually, I started going to church and was amazed at how often the service spoke into my life. The first night I walked into church without a wedding, christening, or funeral to motivate me, I was at my wit's end. We had done the twelve-week feeding program the previous year but I just couldn't sustain it on my own. I was having a bad run with William's eating. I was feeling like a complete and utter failure and that I had no-one to blame but myself. William seemed to be eating less and less and all the gains we had made (however microscopic) were rapidly disappearing. I had all the skills and knowledge that I was ever going to get and I still couldn't do it. I was backed into a corner, fighting a battle I didn't have the strength for. I was depressed and burnt out. My cup wasn't just empty. It was bone dry.

Kylie had been gently offering invitations to church, and church-related events, but the timing was always off. I wanted to go and I promised myself that the next time she invited me I would say 'yes'. Then she rang me early that afternoon and asked if I would like to go to the night service with her. I panicked and promptly said, "No."

I was having a really rough day. The house was a mess. I hadn't given any thought to dinner, and I felt feral and out of control. I didn't want her to see me in that state. Then I remembered what I had promised myself, and I started to give it some proper thought. I rang Kylie back, and told her that I had changed my mind, and would she please pick me up and take me to church.

I was so nervous. I felt a bit like a spy in an enemy camp. The singing was alright, but there were a few lyrics that worried me about this God being better than everyone else's god. I shrugged it off, wanting to keep an open mind and I'm so glad I did. The theme of the message was about winning the unwinnable battle (sound familiar?). The Battle of Jericho was an unwinnable battle. God's people (the Israelites) didn't have the numbers or the weapons. But before the battle started, God sent an angel to meet with the leader of the Israelite army, a man named Joshua. The speaker explained that this let Joshua know that he was not alone in his battle. He didn't have to conquer Jericho in his own strength, because God would be with him. The angel gave him some pretty strange instructions: march around the city once a day for six days, and on the seventh day, march around the city seven times, with the priests blowing the trumpets. All the people had to do was exactly what God told them to do, which, without wanting to sound critical, had to be the worst battle plan in the history of the world. But, lo and behold, it worked. The walls of Jericho crumbled and the city was theirs for the taking. They hadn't needed to fight. They had just had to trust and obey.

Much to my embarrassment, I found myself crying. I was crying because, for such a long time, I had tried to fight this battle on my own. I so desperately wanted William to be able to eat like everyone else, and to go to the toilet like everyone else, but I was tired, so tired of trying to make it happen. And here was this lovely, funny man telling me that I wasn't alone, that 'someone' was with me and I didn't have to fight this battle; all I had to do was trust and let go of the idea that I had to do it all myself.

I felt such a strong sense of relief. I felt the sense of a great and heavy burden being lifted from my shoulders. I felt free to fall and free to fail, because I knew at that moment that William would survive. All I had to do was to keep him alive, one day at a time. The rest had always been out of my control. But for the first time I felt okay about my helplessness. I felt at peace.

Suddenly, what I had once considered the ridiculous ideas of the religious few became plausible. The Bible, which had made little, if any, sense to me before, became not only understandable, but also food for my soul. I had lived my life thinking that the universe was random, but I read in the thin leaf pages of my Bible that the universe was a deliberate act of creation. And that I was neither random nor a burden, but made on purpose, with great love. So there it was… the hope I had needed to fight those dark thoughts that threatened my existence. There might be a point to my average, ordinary, unexceptional little life after all.

I have had to revise my earlier opinions about people of faith, especially Christians. It turns out that they are not all hypocrites and charlatans. Many of them are just really nice and really real people: people who have suffered, people who have prospered, people who have made mistakes, people who have given freely of their time, their talents and resources to bring a little hope and a lot of love to a world in crisis.

I still have objections. There are still a few 'Christian' ideas that I struggle with. I'm okay with that because the God I discovered through the Bible doesn't want blind followers. The Bible has taught me that God wants me to be wise, to use the intellect that he gave me, to think, to ponder, to disagree and to challenge, just as much as he wants me to love and be kind and show mercy.

In the beginning I struggled with my faith on a daily basis. I would constantly ask myself how I could possibly believe, and then I would remember the hopelessness I had felt before and think, 'How could I not?'

I still don't understand the universe (crazy... I know). I still struggle with my depression and anxiety, but I'm seeking help for both of these now. Dealing with William's Autism and SPD still overwhelms me occasionally and leaves me wondering if I will ever feel that I'm doing a good job. But it's different now. There has been a subtle and tenuous shift from hopelessness to hopefulness.

I have started to wonder if that awful black hole that opens at my feet and calls me to fall in might actually just be grief. Grief that my life doesn't measure up to the perfect Hollywood version that lives in my head. Grief that bad things happen to good people. Grief for the sick, the abused, the homeless, the broken. Grief that this world is not as it should be. I used to be afraid of that kind of grief. I thought it would consume me, crush me. Faith in something, *someone*, bigger than I can dream or imagine gives me hope that all this suffering might not be in vain and that one day all will be made right.

As I said at the start of this chapter, I am not an expert on faith. I fully expect that some will read this chapter and dismiss it as nonsense and that is totally fine. It's not my job to change anyone's mind. But to leave this chapter out would be to lie by omission. The peace and acceptance I have found didn't come from me, they came from the One who said, "Come to me, all you who are weary and heavy laden and I will give you rest" (Matthew 11.28).

Questions

It feels kind of awkward to ask you questions here, like I'm trespassing on private property – poking around in your most personal belongings. Maybe instead I could ask you to pause and think about what you've just read and how it made you feel. And, regardless of where you sit on the subject of faith, I hope that you know that you are loved and supported. I hope that you know that you don't have to fight this battle on your own.

14

Don't Forget About your Daughter, Dear!

I'm not sure if I've made it obvious but I also have a daughter: the other pea in our family pod. On two separate occasions, when I was chatting to new-found acquaintances about my concerns with William, they both kindly cautioned me not to forget my daughter. Both times I was a bit perplexed. Why would they say that? And why was I perplexed? Shouldn't I be offended? Then I worked it out. I realised that they were cautioning me because they didn't know her. If they knew Rachael, they wouldn't feel the need to caution me. They'd make me a cup of tea and find me a chocolate biscuit and maybe some Valium. Joking!

My daughter is lovely, sensitive and challenging, but she also happens to be intensely private. I discovered this by mistake when I posted something she had done onto social media. It was so cute! But when my friend casually mentioned it to Rachael, she was horrified. I can still feel her hurt and accusing eyes burning into mine. How did this friend of mine know about [that thing that shall not be mentioned]?

I thought she raised a valid point. I was also more than a little bit chastised that my then five-year-old daughter had more sense than her mother. Posting my daughter's private life on social media, indeed! Who did I think I was? Since then I have rarely shared anything about the kids on social media and never without their express permission, which is why I have deliberately kept Rachael out of this story as much as possible. At the same time, I know there will be people out there who are concerned for this seemingly overlooked child. So let me take a moment to reassure you that Rachael is not overlooked. Rachael would not *allow* herself to be overlooked, and for that I am very grateful. It makes my job a little bit easier, knowing that she will let me know loudly and clearly if she is ever in danger of being overlooked.

However, this does bring up an important point. A balance needs to be found. An equity must exist across members of the family unit for love and attention. Husbands, wives and children all need to feel valued, important, seen and heard. This isn't easy in any family and is made infinitely more challenging when you throw in additional needs, whatever those needs might be. Sometimes I do give more of my attention to William, but there are times too when Rachael gets more of me. Michael and I have needs as well, but mercifully we are both fairly low maintenance adults, and so long as he can have some uninterrupted screen time and I can have time out with friends, we plod along quite nicely.

Sometimes there's not a lot of choice about who gets the most attention when one of us actually just needs more. Those times can't be helped (trips to emergency, specialist appointments and therapy) but once the crisis has passed I know that it's time to swing back in another direction. We don't always get the balance right. I make mistakes. I say sorry and I try to do better. And I think it's not a bad thing for our children (and each other) to know that we are human.

We aren't magicians, or super heroes or time travellers, but we can say sorry when it's needed and we can try to do better when we muck things up. So, yes, I do make time for Rachael, and Michael, and myself. And I am thankful to those people who gently remind me to keep my finger on that particular pulse.

You may also wonder what effect William's fussy eating has had on Rachael's eating. How does a parent make such dramatic compromises for one child and not the other? The truth is I haven't. Rachael is afforded the same privileges as William, and she is not forced to eat food she doesn't like. I can't see how it would be fair. Luckily for me, Rachael actually likes a much broader range of foods than William does. She loves fruit. She will eat bread and pasta. She eats meat. She isn't a huge fan of vegetables but eats enough for me to be fairly confident that, as she matures, she will develop a taste for a variety of healthy foods. Unlike William, she doesn't scream or run away, which is nice. She doesn't always eat what Mike and I eat, and I have become adept at making her a separate meal. I would much prefer to make three different meals and have peace than have a battle. That is my choice. Other families must make decisions that suit them and their needs.

Rachael and William are best friends and worst enemies. Having a brother with Autism and Sensory Processing Disorder isn't always easy for her. There's not much I can do about that except be a listening post and a soft place to land when things get rough. It stresses me out sometimes, trying to keep the peace, trying not to make Rachael do all of the compromising, trying not to expect too much emotional maturity from her. This stress increases when they are fighting with each other. But I was granted a moment of clarity one day not that long ago.

We were running late for school and I was frustrated by my inability to be more organised. Tensions were high. The kids had gone down to the car while I finished locking up the house. By the time I reached them, they had had a major fight. Harsh words had been spoken. Hearts had been broken. It seemed that Autism was receiving the blame. I know that they wouldn't like me to share the details but it had to do with not accepting each other and not making allowances for each other. William finds it very difficult to make any kind of compromise. Rachael — who is very generous with her efforts to get along and smooth the path — was frustrated by his inability to reciprocate. All I could think was, 'I don't have time for this rubbish', followed by a string of unspoken expletives. I tried my best to calm the waters, to smooth the ruffled feathers, but we live too close to the school and this fight needed more than five minutes to be resolved. A multitude of depressing thoughts flooded my brain. I just wanted to raise children who would be kind to each other but, on this day, it seemed that I had failed.

I was fighting back tears of frustration as I walked the kids into school. We walked past another brother and sister being unkind to each other. And when I walked into Rachael's classroom I found the teacher telling off a group of students who had apparently not been very kind to another group of students. As I drove home, I had time to process what had happened and to realise that it wasn't Autism that was the problem. It was just a brother and sister thing. It was a human thing.

Disagreements, arguments, harsh words, hurt feelings and fights would happen whether William had Autism or not. And as much as I dislike it when they are at odds with each other, I have come to see that it is a necessary part of growing up. They must both learn to disagree in healthy ways. They must learn to speak up for and defend themselves and others. And they must learn what harm can be caused when they hurt others through thoughtless or malicious actions, and the importance of appropriately expressing their tempers. I just needed to remind myself that they are actually doing a pretty good job.

Rachael is an amazing kid. I love her more than I can say. I'm proud of her spirit, her talents and her strength, even though they have a tendency to wear me out. I might get distracted and there may be times when she has to remind me to give her my full attention but you may rest easy. I'm not likely to forget that I have a daughter any time soon.

Questions

Do you have more than one child?

Do you struggle to find a balance in the attention you give to each member of the family?

Would you benefit from respite?

Do you know what local agencies (if any) provide respite for children with special needs?

Do you have a friend or relative who would be willing to help with respite?

15

Learning to Live a Life Less Worried

This has not been an easy journey, but I can honestly say that life at the moment is pretty sweet. And one of the main reasons that I think life is so good is that (apart from the fact that all of our basic needs are being met, including sleep and personal space) I am learning to let go of worry. Accepting that I am a perfectionist with intermittent depression and generalised anxiety disorder has been a huge part of this process. I'm no longer fighting it or hiding it or denying it. I am seeking help to manage it. I can be honest with myself and about myself. Of course I still withhold the absolute truth occasionally, and tell people "I'm fine" when I'm not. But that's only when it would be socially awkward to say, "Actually..." and drench them in a verbal outpouring of all my woes.

Seeing Karren on a regular basis, the lucky recipient of most of my verbal outpourings, really helped me to change my 'stinking thinking', as she called it. She listened with compassion and empathy. She helped me to make sense of the chaos in my brain. My brain is full of 'stuff', not all of it good, but not all of it rubbish either. She helped me to learn how to sort through it all; to make decisions about what's worth keeping and what's not. She validated the challenges in my life and reassured me that I'm doing the best I can with what I have. She helped to give me strategies so that when challenges crop up I can handle them on my own. She discharged me (if that's the right term), and it would seem that I am right for now. But I know that she is always just a phone call away if I really need her.

I hardly ever panic about William's eating any more. And most of the time I'm able to talk about his eating issues openly, without feeling guilty that I'm not doing more to help him. Of course there is more that could be done, but right now I'm comfortable with the level of attention I give to his nutritional needs. He looks healthy. He has enough energy to be a kid, to play and have fun. He is doing pretty well at school and at home. And just at the moment, I think that this is enough. I'm well aware that not everyone agrees with me on this point. And there are times that I convince myself that I could give it one more shot. When I have conversations with friends and family, and describe William's eating issues, it's easy to assuage their concern by convincing them and myself that I could have another go at improving William's diet. Maybe one day I'll surprise myself and actually do it. But for now my anxiety, my perfectionism (that demands all or nothing) and the mountain of sensory issues that need to be overcome defeat me. So I grieve. I grieve that I cannot do better. But I do so now without the panic and with as much compassion for myself as I can find.

Letting go of the worry has been easier since I realised that if William had diabetes instead of Sensory Processing Disorder, I wouldn't think it was my fault. I wouldn't think my bad parenting had caused his condition. I wouldn't think it was my job to cure him. I'm sure that I would be sad and frustrated by the complications that Diabetes brings, but I would know that my job would start and finish with management. And so, since that revelation, I have tried to concern myself with managing William's eating difficulties, not curing them. It's been suggested by friends that I get regular blood tests for William, for my peace of mind. But the few blood tests that William has experienced were far too traumatic to repeat without a specific reason. So I monitor his general health and promise to get him to the doctor if his health declines. I talk to him about how he needs to think about looking after himself, about making sure he has enough energy to do all the busy and important jobs of being a kid, like growing and playing and having fun.

He hears the constant message of 'healthy eating' from school and so I temper it with talking about the healthiest foods that William likes to eat. I tell him that peanut paste on rice cakes is a pretty healthy option for him. Sometimes I suggest that if he's really concerned about eating healthy food he could always try an apple. I confess that I do this mostly for entertainment; his reactions of horror and disgust are just too good to resist. But I guess I also do it because maybe, just maybe, he'll surprise me with a 'yes'.

I have accepted that there are going to be times when William's eating difficulties will cause problems like at school, in restaurants, on school camps and on holidays, or anytime we leave home. I'm getting better at dealing with these complications and finding solutions that are respectful of William's right to dignity.

I'm getting better at talking to teachers, school staff, friends and relatives about what William needs. This isn't my favourite thing to do. I would much prefer to bury my head in the sand and pretend that everything will turn out for the best. Sometimes I do bury my head, and sometimes it does turn out okay. But other times I have collected a very sad boy from school or wherever, and I have pledged to do better next time.

William has come up with his own strategy for dealing with well-meaning people who try to get him to try new foods. He tells them that he is 'allergic'. There are enough kids out there with allergies to all sorts of food, that this is easily accepted, and it gives William power to defend himself when I'm not there. When he first told me, I was a bit horrified that he was lying to people, but then I realised that no one would try to force food on a child who claimed to be 'allergic'. Pretty clever, right?

I have spent most of my life bracing myself for other people's censure, afraid to do the 'wrong' thing. I have felt hemmed in by all the unwritten and constantly changing 'rules' of society. But just recently it occurred to me that we do not live in a fascist state but a free country. Many of the things that have caused me worry have done so, not because I have a problem with them, but because I don't want to be seen to be doing the wrong thing. I don't know why it's taken me so long to work that out.

Despite what popular journalism and social media would have us believe, there are no laws regarding most of the ways I choose to parent my children. There is no law that says I can't feed my children potato chips for dinner, or forgo a bath occasionally (or frequently), or run late for school from time to time. When I can't tolerate the frenetic pace of life or how much pressure my kids are under, I sometimes decide that we all need a mental health day. I don't know what the education authorities call it, but I call it parental discretion. I am after all an adult, and adults get to make decisions (good, bad and indifferent). This might have been obvious to some people, but for me it's joyful and liberating news.

I don't really mean to sound like an anarchist. I'm not anti-government or anti-establishment. It's my job to teach my children to be respectful of themselves, others and property. It's my deepest desire that they will become kind, thoughtful, productive and happy adults. I just didn't realise that by being so worried about what others would think of me, I had been giving my power away. I am my children's mother, and so long as I obey the law and do my best to keep them safe from harm, abuse and neglect then I'm doing okay.

'So what does William eat now?' I hear you ask. Well, until very recently, he was having a chocolate shake (made on Pediasure, ice cream, Milo and Benefibre) for breakfast. Now he has two plain rice cakes spread with peanut paste, which he has for dinner as well. He has a Drumstick mini for dessert. And he eats an assortment of chips, crackers, rice cakes and miscellaneous foodstuffs throughout the day. He also takes Vitamin C and a kid's multivitamin (when we remember). I don't pretend that it is an ideal diet for an eleven-year-old boy. But I contend that it is adequate. And I am at peace with this. I would prefer to let go of the worry and look at the evidence before me, which is a boy who is happy and healthy and loving his perfect life.

{ 16 }

Top Tips

I'd like to end with my top tips for surviving raising an extremely fussy eater.

At some point in my life I realised that advice was a bit like the giveaways people leave on their footpath. Just because someone puts it out there doesn't mean we have to pick it up and take it home. So keeping that in mind, and knowing that you are under no obligation to take it on board, allow me to share some helpful hints, from one parent to another.

Breathe. Just breathe. I wish I had a time machine so that I could go back and tell myself that everything will be okay, but I don't. So I'm telling you. You are not alone. Everything will be okay.

See your doctor (assuming that you haven't already). Make sure that there isn't a physical complication preventing your child from eating. If your doctor cannot find a medical reason consider seeing an Occupational Therapist or Speech Language Pathologist (preferably trained in SOS or other feeding program) and ask them to do an assessment of your child's eating. It won't be cheap and you'll probably be on a waiting list for a while but my guess is that it will prove to be very informative.

Accept that it's not your fault. It's not your fault. *It's not your fault.* You did not create this problem. You do not possess some strange enchanting power that has caused this to happen. You do however have to deal with it, in your own way, and as best as you can. What that looks like will be different for each one of us. And that is absolutely okay.

Call in the professionals. If by some rare and beautiful miracle the stars (availability, time, money) align and you are able to attend an SOS feeding program then do it. Blaming myself was probably the least helpful thing

I had done in all the ups and downs of William's feeding problems. Learning that it wasn't my fault was probably the most powerful thing I gained from doing the feeding program. For that reason alone I think it is worth it.

Accept that it's not your child's fault. They are not trying to manipulate you or control you. They are not being deliberately naughty or disobedient. They are learning a skill, one that is difficult for them and causing them a great deal of distress. Be kind to them and to yourself.

Accept that people will say idiotic things. They won't mean to, but they'll do it anyway. They will give you unsolicited advice. Sometimes it will be useful, mostly it won't be. Eventually you may begin to see these interactions as a chance to advocate for your child and children like them. Until then my only suggestion is to nod, smile and change the subject.

Separate the eating of food from the process of learning to eat. Of course our kids need to eat. Their bodies need fuel to grow and perform essential functions like brain activity and breathing and stuff. But they also need to learn to engage with food. Some kids can do this at the same time. Try not to be upset if yours cannot. Feed them but also give them space to learn about eating. Progress, not perfection.

Accept that junk food is not the enemy. Junk food can be a useful stepping stone (a stepping stone William hasn't yet moved on from, but guess what? He's still alive and doing quite well). Ideally our children will progress to eating a balanced diet from a broad range of foodstuffs. But while they are learning, a small range of simple and familiar foods will support your child's nutritional needs. These foods may or may not include junk food, and that's okay.

Accept that food is morally neutral. Food is neither good nor bad. Foods are simply compounds made up of different nutrients. Our bodies don't care that Sally from down the road only feeds her children locally sourced, organic wholefoods. The human body is incredibly resourceful in its ability to squeeze every last morsel of usable matter from the food we consume. Feed your children as best you can, but trust in their bodies to make the most of it. Multivitamins and supplements can be useful for bridging nutritional gaps. I strongly advise doing this with the help of doctor or other qualified health professional (such as a dietician). This can be very difficult with children with sensory issues. Finding anything ingestible that they will accept can feel nigh on impossible. Keep trying but try not to let it stress you out.

Relax and reframe your understanding of health and nutrition. Is your child otherwise healthy and well? Do they have enough energy to do all the important jobs of childhood, like growing and playing and learning and having fun? It's a bit gross but are they doing a healthy number of wees and poos? And are their poos bulky and moist and pass easily? If the answer to these questions is yes, then great! Take a moment to celebrate the awesomeness of good health and regular bowel movements. If the answers were no, then I'm sorry, but don't feel like you have to solve all these issues on your own. Talk to the professionals, make sure that they *hear* you, and demand/insist that they find creative ways to solve any immediate or urgent needs your child might have. If the person you are receiving advice from can't or won't help you, then ask to see someone who can. Don't let them put all the pressure on you, remind yourself that if there was an easy fix to these problems you would have solved them already. (Easier said than done, I know).

Develop a support network. You need people who are supportive and understanding and non-judgemental. This doesn't have to be a huge group. Even just one or two people can make a big difference. You need people who will celebrate all the awesome things about your child, who will encourage you and cheer you on when you think you can't take even one more step. People who will remind you of how awesome you are and how much hard work you put in every single day. Find them online if you can't find them in real life. I promise you that they do exist.

Take care of yourself. No! Really, I mean it. Take care of yourself. Who will take care of your children if you are burnt out and used up? I'm not even going to offer any suggestions — you know what this looks like for you. Just take a moment to give it some proper thought. Given all the obstacles that are standing in your way what would really and truly help you to relax? Given all the constraints and restrictions on your time and resources what would really and truly recharge your battery? Only you know. Only you can make it happen.

Check your [m]ental hygiene! What are most of your thoughts like? Happy and positive? Depressed, angry and/or negative? Do you feel like a failure? If you are feeling like you can barely keep your head above water, then maybe it's time to see your doctor. You don't have to wait until you have a complete mental breakdown to get a little help. You'd take your car to a mechanic for a service, wouldn't you? Why not take your brain to a psychologist? Just a thought...

Finally, I want to thank you for coming on this journey with me. I hope that I have done our story justice. Please remember that I am not an expert. Everything in this book is based on either my experience or the things that I have read or been told along the way. They are intended to be helpful and thought provoking but are not intended to replace medical advice. I hope you have found it helpful or, at the very least, that it's given you pause to consider what it might be like to raise a child with extremely fussy eating.

Appendix One

Recommended Reading

I love reading and learning. I would not be the (mostly) calm and rational parent I am today without the instructions and insights of many thought-provoking authors. The following is a list of books that I have found to be both informative and encouraging. I realise that most of them are about Autism or Sensory Processing Disorder. Your child may not have Autism or Sensory Processing Disorder, but if your child is an extremely fussy eater I think you might find at least some of these books interesting.

The Out of Sync Child, by Carol Stock Kranowitz, M.A. (Penguin Putnam Inc, 2006). This book gave me an excellent insight into Sensory Processing Disorder. Specifically, it helped me to understand William and his sensory needs a whole better. And generally, it helped me to understand people better.

Can't Eat, Won't Eat, by Brenda Legge (Jessica Kingsley, 2008). The only book I've been able to find that has even come close to matching my experience with trying to get an extremely fussy eater to eat. This book is based on anecdotal research as well as the author's personal experience with her own son.

The Australian Autism Handbook, by Benison O'Reilly and Seana Smith (Jane Curry Publishing, 2008). Written by a couple of Aussie mums who were frustrated at the lack of information out there for Australian parents of children on the spectrum. There are so many great stories in this book. It is thoroughly informative, but also heart-warming and hopeful.

Ten Things Every Child With Autism Wishes You Knew, by Ellen Notbohm (Future Horizons Inc., 2005). An impressively insightful book written by the mother of a child on the spectrum from the perspective of her child. This is a book for everyone but especially useful for teachers and grandparents, who want to understand but just can't get their heads around these beautiful yet perplexing children.

The Child with Special Needs, by Stanley I. Greenspan, M.D. and Serena Wieder, PH.D. with Robin Simons (Da Capo Press, 1998). This is one of the more academic books on this list, not always easy to read, but I read it as an introduction to DIR®/Floortime™. This book challenges the reader to look beyond the label, to see the child and how best to engage with them in a way that helps them rather than dismisses them. If you don't mind something a bit weightier, it's well worth the read.

Dear Gabriel, by Halfdan W. Freihow (House of Anansi Pr, 2008). This book made me weep. It is so simply, beautifully and powerfully written. A dad's heartfelt letter to his Autistic son. This is a book full of a father's confusion, frustrations, love and compassion. It is poetic, raw and emotional, and I loved it. Probably best read if you've been walking this walk for a while.

Love, Tears & Autism, by Cecily Paterson (Ark House Press and Media Incorporated, 2011). An Australian mum writes candidly about her struggles with raising a child on the spectrum within the context of her Christian faith. It is beautifully and eloquently written. I beg you not to let any prejudice you might have against Christianity prevent you from reading this book; it would be a great shame to miss out on this treasure, in my opinion.

The Little Book of Anxiety: Confessions from a Worried Life, by Kerri Sackville (Random House Australia, 2012). I loved this book. Right from its opening chapter I was captivated by this woman's ability to use her personal experience to help me understand my own anxiety.

Oh, the Places You'll Go! By Dr Seuss (Random House, 1990). That man was a genius! This story saved my life. Yes, I know it's a kid's story. Just read it. It won't take you long and you'll feel so much better about your life. I promise.

So there you go. Nine books that have helped me along the way. If you get the chance to read them I hope you enjoy them as much as I did.

Appendix Two

Notes for Paediatrician

These are the notes that I prepared for our first consultation with the paediatrician regarding our concern over William's development.

Parents: Michael (42) and Shannon (30) Thiry
Siblings: Rachael Thiry (3)

William was delivered by Caesarean at 39½ weeks due to breech position, no other complications during pregnancy or birth.

We had difficulties with breastfeeding, problems with attachment and supply. At two and a half weeks he had failed to gain weight. I was given Motilium and told to complement feeds with formula. He seemed to have a 'lazy' suck, even on the bottle. Breastfeeding didn't really improve and my milk disappeared at around three months. He never really attempted to hold the bottle himself.

He started rolling over at about three months, and crawling at about six months.

He never looked comfortable sitting up – preferred to be on his knees as he got older.

Walked at 17 months, but had been shuffling on his knees for several months before this.

I attempted to introduce rice cereal at five months but he refused. He accepted rice cereal at six months and pureed food shortly after, but refused lumpier food when I tried to introduce it from about nine months. For a while I could get him to eat small amounts of peas and fish fingers but I gave up in frustration at about 18 months. He has not eaten meat since then and a very limited amount of vegetables (fresh snow peas when grown in our garden). He has an overreaction when food is offered to him that he doesn't want. He now eats mainly dry cereal, rice cakes with peanut butter/Nutella/honey, flavoured rice cakes, milk, biscuits, cheese and crackers, and ice-cream. The only fruit he has eaten since 18 months is fresh lychees.

He started babbling at what seemed a normal age but didn't start using recognisable words until after 24 months. At the age of three he was referred to speech pathology through Community Health. About six months later, William was assessed by a visiting speech pathologist from Rockhampton. She told us that, while William was in need of speech therapy, there was no-one in Gladstone to provide it.

Community Health contacted me early in 2009 offering speech therapy, which we accepted. William's speech improved and we stopped going. I asked to be kept on the books and we went again later in the year; at this time he was assessed as having speech at or about his age level and we were discharged. Although his Kindergarten teacher maintained that he still had difficulties with expressive speech, I was relieved that the speech therapist had cleared William.

At his four year health check, he was referred to the Child Assessment Team. We saw the physiotherapist; she assessed William as being in the normal range. We saw the occupational therapist in November 2009, who assessed William as needing some help; unfortunately she would soon be on maternity leave and was unsure of what services would be available. I have not been contacted by them again. We sought therapy through a private OT, at the beginning of 2010, she identified that William had low tone, proprioception and oral defensiveness. We have stopped going because of the expense and I felt embarrassed at not managing to maintain the home program she had written for us.

William experienced night terrors from about two and a half to three (I'm guessing) and sometimes still has bad dreams.

Problematic behaviours:

Fussy eating and overreaction to food being offered to him. He held a grudge against his father for two weeks because Michael tried to get him to eat a grape; William still doesn't like Michael to prepare his food.

Writing – poor handwriting, difficulty holding pencil, has shown almost no interest in drawing/writing until prep. He is improving all the time but is still well behind his peers.

Moving – he looks awkward when trying to negotiate playground equipment, especially climbing over A-frames. At cross country earlier this year he was about 75m behind the second last child over a 200m course.

Swimming – he has trouble coordinating his arms, kicking and breathing, even though he has no fear of the water and has been receiving swimming lessons since about 18 months of age.

Dribbling – he often dribbles when he is absorbed in a task or watching TV.

Toilet training — he is still not fully toilet trained. He wets his pants frequently and sometimes soils them. He is still in a night nappy.

Chewing non-food items – this began last year with the bottom of his shirt and his collar, now he constantly chews on his hat string, and often his toys.

Hand flapping when excited and upset – this started at the same time as knee shuffling; until now I thought it was just a 'quirk'.

Limited expressive language — if he has lots of words to get out they seem to get tangled.

Lives in his own world — doesn't seem to be aware of what's happening around him, seems to lack curiosity, and is usually unfazed by change.

At school engages in mostly parallel play but becomes more collaborative with his sister who is sixteen months younger.

Has difficulty following instructions, especially regarding moving his body in a specific way (arms by your side, roll onto your belly, etc)

Gets upset easily but will mostly settle easily.

Has difficulty sitting still, and difficulty maintaining attention. (He doesn't usually misbehave but will constantly change his position and often looks around the classroom).

Has difficulty sitting on my lap; he seems to slide off unless I am reclined.

His father and I were both a little odd growing up, so we have embraced William's quirks as a unique part of his personality. But now that he is at school with 20 peers, it has become obvious that he will require more assistance than the average child if he is to remain engaged and experience success in his education.

Things that are great:

William is happy and affectionate.
He has a sense of humour, likes playing tricks and being cheeky.

He smiles and laughs readily.

He is enjoying learning his letters and numbers even though he has trouble writing them.

He talks about his friends at school and likes to make things for them.

Acknowledgements

No man is an island. And it seems that this book isn't one either. I might have written it but it contains the lives, thoughts and ideas of many people. Not only that but many people have also breathed life into it along the way. Those people have guided and encouraged me, been kind to me and challenged me. So to those people I'd like to say a very heartfelt thank you.

To Janet Thornthwaite, whose very kind donation of time and talents dragged my early writing into something worthy of being read. Also, for her gracious hospitality, I loved our chats over a cup of tea and a scone.

To my editor, Cecily Paterson, for knocking off the rough edges and adding the polish. And also for her help in getting this book off my computer screen and into real life. Words really aren't enough.

To the friends and family (you know who you are) who read my early manuscripts and whose feedback and encouragement have helped me to overcome the anxiety of putting myself out there.

To Michael, my darling husband, who might not always show his encouragement in ways that I can easily understand, but I am learning. I couldn't have published this without your support, so thank you for supporting me and this book, even though it wasn't your cup of tea.

To Rachael, the loveliest of lovely daughters, you inspire and challenge me daily. Thank you for being you.

To William, for being the amazing, generously spirited kid that you are. I'm not sure what I would have done if you hadn't given me permission to publish our story, but I am awfully glad I didn't need to find out. And just for the record, it's I who loves you more.

About the Author

Shannon Thiry is a stay-at-home mum, which she
loves when she's not too busy complaining about how
much she hates housework. She's married to Michael
and they have two awesome children, William and
Rachael. They live in Queensland, Australia. They
live a very ordinary life, getting away to visit family
and friends when they can, but mostly just hanging
out at home, enjoying the serenity. Ha!

Shannon writes about parenting, advocating
and fussy eating at **www.shannonthiry.com**

CPSIA information can be obtained
at www.ICGtesting.com
Printed in the USA
BVHW070948091121
621174BV00006B/100